I0160359

MOTIVATIONAL

REFLECTIONS

– AT SUNSET

BY

DR. ROCCO LEONARD MARTINO

PUBLISHED BY

BlueNose
PRESS, INC.

PRINTED IN THE UNITED STATES OF AMERICA
PUBLISHED JUNE 2018

Cover Design: Joseph A. Martino
Interior Layout Design: Joseph A. Martino

For more information on this title please visit:
www.BlueNosePress.com

DEDICATION

I dedicate this book to my wife Barbara. We have been married almost 57 years. How she has put up with me for so long is quite a miracle. God bless her. I love her so much.

ACKNOWLEDGEMENTS

A book of this nature cannot be written without the support of many people. As I wrote, many friends from the past, some no longer with us, whispered in my ear "Remember when..."

With deep appreciation to Tom Burgoyne, Kevin Callahan, Paul Peterson, Albert Tegler, and Rev. George W. Bur, SJ for writing reviews about *Motivational Reflections – At Sunset.*

I appreciate the efforts of Christine Monigle who was instrumental in transcribing my dictations, and Treecee Polgar for editing my structures, and commenting on my ideas.

I also would like to thank my second son, Joseph, for designing the cover and preparing this book for publication.

My deepest thanks to all of you.

REVIEWS

Dr. Martino's *Motivational Reflections – At Sunset* will encourage those of us in the last quarter or fifth of life to revive a youthful curiosity about our multi-dimensional world. This curiosity Dr. Martino never lost through his long life. Readers will especially enjoy his grateful testimony about the miracle that cured his cancer and about his hope that the new technologies of the 21st Century will create opportunities for us to refocus on faith and family.

He continues to express himself like a teacher always as he writes "to impact young minds." Yes, the young as well as the old, will use his reflections on his life and on topics of the present day to help form their own opinions. All will find, in addition, an incentive in these pages to imitate Dr. Martino. Expressing in writing one's opinions about the topics of the day is so engaging as to focus and energize the spirits of both a distracted youth and a diminishing elder.

- Rev. George W. Bur, SJ, Superior of the Jesuit Center in Wernersville, PA

Rocky Martino has fit a million lives into one amazing life. *Motivational Reflections - At Sunset* beautifully chronicles his triumphs and a few regrets but also gives us a blueprint on how we should care for one another and enjoy every sunset.

Rocky is the inventor of the smartphone. He made a life surfing the wave of technology, so his plea to "use technology, don't be afraid of it" is perfectly predictable. Not so predictable was Rocky's suggestion that we throw all the smartphones in a pile, light them on fire and use the smoke to send smoke signals to communicate with one another. That way, he states, maybe people will start talking to each other again instead of being glued to their devises and civility might return to society. He has spent his life trying to make the world a better place and with *Motivational Reflections - At Sunset,* he continues on that quest.

- Tom Burgoyne, The Best Friend of the Phillie Phanatic and Co-Author of Pheel the Love!

Motivational Reflections - At Sunset is such a wonderful and inspirational read that Dr. Martino's latest book should be read before the "sunset" years.

There are so many life lessons gained through the author's experience and living. His words serve as wise fatherly advice for any age. Certainly, there is a lifetime to learn from this fascinating man who studied at the Vatican Library and the Jerusalem

Library of Biblical Studies, including the value of writing daily, which he has done in completing 28 non-fiction books, five novels and one play as well as his three-volume autobiography.

Indeed, Dr. Martino is a smart man, after all he invented the smartphone. Be wise and take time to read these antidotes and advice on living and life as they will not only make you want to be a better person but give you a path. Truly, any reader of any age will learn from someone who is so learned and especially those watching the sunset.

- Kevin Callahan, Sports Writer and Author of The Black Rose, The Fish Finder, and The Chess Game

The singular advantage of becoming older is the ongoing acquisition of wisdom. Its disadvantage is living in a world that is inexorably becoming smaller.

It does not have to be so. *Motivational Reflections – At Sunset* is an expansion of Doctor Martino's world to include you and me. His wise insights gleaned from a long life lived well, should be shared. I am glad he has; so will you, his reader. And, you will be encouraged to do the same.

- Paul C. Peterson, P.E., Fellow of the American Society of Civil Engineers, Retired Chair of the

Theology Department at Bishop Shanahan High School, Downingtown, PA

Motivational Reflections – At Sunset is an interesting and informative book. Reading the book gives one the feeling of having a pleasant and insightful conversation with an old friend.

Rocky Martino gives us a view of the world as he has known it over the past eight plus decades and a view of the world as he sees it in the future. His grasp of the events of the past 89 years is extensive and presented in a very enjoyable manner.

The future he presents should give ample food for thought and hope for a better world to come.

I highly recommend reading this book.

- Albert W. Tegler, President & CEO, Tegler Benefits Group

WORKS BY ROCCO LEONARD MARTINO

FICTION

The Cross of Victory

Christianity: A Criminal Investigation...

The Resurrection: A Criminal Investigation...

9-11-11: The Tenth Anniversary Attack

The Plot to Cancel Christmas

NONFICTION

The Coming Technology Tsunami

Memories: Volume I - Stories for My Grandchildren

Memories: Volume II - Scientist and Writer

Memories: Volume III - Changing the World

Rocket Ships and God

People, Machines, and Politics of the Cyber Age Creation

Finding the Critical Path

Applied Operational Planning

Allocating and Scheduling Resources

Critical Path Networks

Resources Management

Dynamic Costing

Project Management

Decision Patterns

Decision Tables with Staff of MDI

Information Management

Integrated Manufacturing Systems

Management Information Systems

MIS Methodology

Personnel Management Systems

IMPACT 70s with John Gentile

TABLE OF CONTENTS

PREFACE

Did I succeed in using all the talents given to me at birth? What did I accomplish? How? Why?

The calendar says I am 89, but my stamina, will, heart, and spirit say I am still 21. What a dichotomy. I can still do most of the routine in the gym, even if I don't breathe as easily as I finish. In fact, I am often gasping. The treadmill is harder and harder to push, but I can still go full bore. It is the bike that gives me a problem. I must continually adjust the depth of the pedals on the bike. I refuse to admit that I am 89 and not 21.

The exercise part of the gym is no problem to my body; but my spirits often strike a low point. The worst part of the gym is that I am usually alone. My buddies are all gone, my sons are busy with their careers and raising their own children, and my wife was never a gym girl. The grim reaper seems to be standing by, waiting for me to falter.

Getting old is both a blessing and a curse. The blessing lies in the children. It's great to see the grandchildren and great grandchildren growing up, going through the same stages of life as our own children. We had four boys and great times going through their different levels of development,

1

schooling, college, and early career days. We built models together, did Scouts, and I was often the coach of their sports teams. They grew up too soon! Peter graduated from the Naval Academy, was commissioned and went to sea as a submarine officer. I lived his danger with him knowing far too much after my four years as a consultant to the Pentagon. I shared the joys and triumphs of all four boys, and I shared their low points when things went awry, as they always do — Paul as a White House intern, John as a Senate intern, Joe in Wheeling, West Virginia, studying for a double master's degree. The highs and lows were exhilarating and being part of their lives was a joy beyond belief. I was wanted. I was needed. As their children grew up, I became a consultant, someone to ask for advice or counsel. Hopefully, I didn't intrude. This brought back memories of my father. A voice on the other end of the telephone giving the advice I asked for. So, the cycle of life repeats itself. I seem to be on the last cycle.

One curse of old age is the loss of friends. Some were priests and I miss having Mass said around the breakfast table or around the coffee table in the living room. I miss praying quietly with a friend. The conversations were often deep and rewarding. Two of my ordained buddies were bishops, three were cardinals. Our conversations were positive, open, and supportive. We shared our ideas, our problems, and our lives. They are all gone, and I am lonely. Now I talk to them in prayer and I believe they hear me.

The loss of friends is almost matched by my inability to pick up and fly anywhere in the world. First, I must check to see if dialysis is available at the planned destination and if they have an open slot for me. If available, often I must modify my schedule. Sometimes, I must cancel my plans. But at least I can still travel despite the need for dialysis everywhere. My kidneys are shot due to anesthesia from thirteen surgeries tied to bladder cancer, which I have beaten. It is gone. But it took my kidney function with it.

How old am I? I am 89. I will be 100 in eleven short years. I know I will make it. I wonder how far beyond 100 I will get. Right now, it is a scorecard. Some people need a scorecard of their fortune. Not me. I gave it away. My scorecard is my final age. My grandmother made it to 96. My great-grandfather made it to 98. I want to beat them both.

So, I am chronologically old. So what! Apropos of nothing at all, I want to go skiing this winter.

By the strangest of circumstances, although I don't see it that way, the morning after I wrote this piece, our youngest son John sent me a text message. It reads:

> "It is not true that people stop pursuing dreams because they grow old, they grow old because they stop pursuing dreams."
> — *Gabriel Garcia Marques*

I still dream of doing things. I am going back into business because I have an idea for a new product. I think it will do quite well. It is needed.

Why this anthology of essays? They might be interesting to you. I feel strongly about some things and laugh at many more. I hope you will join me in the hidden laughter in most of these pieces. I love life, I love people, and I love to be happy. Even in the direst of situations, I would laugh. I agree with Ella Wheeler Wilcox when she wrote, "Laugh and the world laughs with you; weep and you weep alone."

Most importantly, I never quit. I refuse to get old. I refuse to stop. This book will show you how. Age is a relative thing. Don't give in to the years.

I do sit and think a lot. I enjoy solving problems that bugged me when I was young. This book will tell you all about them. I like to ponder and reflect — especially at sunset. After all, this is the sunset of my life.

I love sunsets, the sheer beauty from the flight deck of an aircraft over the Atlantic or Pacific is breathtaking. Even more so in the Artic with the Aurora Borealis – the Northern Lights.

Sunsets are the harbinger of hope. With anticipation we look forward to the sunrise of another day. And one day there will be a new sunrise that will last forever.

But until then, let's live!

FAITH

"First of all, you ask me if the God of Christians
forgives one who doesn't believe and doesn't seek
the faith. Premise that – and it's the fundamental
thing – the mercy of God has no limits if one
turns to him with a sincere and contrite heart;
the question for one who doesn't believe in
God lies in obeying one's conscience."
— Pope Francis

Faith is usually connected with religious
belief. As a matter of fact, faith can be connected to
anything, whether religious or not. For example, we
have tremendous faith when we board an airplane
that it will not only take off, but then fly safely to its
planned destination. That faith is a belief and an
acceptance of the concept of aeronautics even if we
cannot understand it. While aeronautical engineers
can understand why an airplane can fly, we as the
general public do not have that information, but we
do have faith in the engineers who have designed
and created the aircraft that it will do as we expect it
to do. In that sense faith is not only belief but
acceptance that the belief is true and worthy of
belief.

There seems to be a great deal of controversy
coming from people who have no faith and no belief

in a supernatural creator, God. The usual complaint is that it is difficult if not impossible if not unreasonable to believe in something that cannot be seen or understood. How ridiculous and small-minded that is.

I happen to be a rocket scientist and hence the mysteries of why an airplane flies and of why a rocket can rise beyond the atmosphere of the Earth is no mystery to me. It is not a question of faith, but in my case, it is one of understanding the equations that regulate the behavior of aircraft and rocket ships. But yet I do not know what gravity is. I know how to work with gravity, or against it, but I do not know what it is. I know what the measurements are. I know what the force characteristics are, but I haven't got a clue as to what gravity really is in its essence other than the fact that it is a force. It is a force associated with a mass. Why? I don't know.

And so, we come to the case of a belief in an infinite and eternal God. Why? I don't know. I have the belief, I have the understanding that there must be a God that created this universe in which the planet Earth is an insignificant part, but I don't know how, and I don't know why. That doesn't change things. My mind says that there must be a God. My spirit accepts it. That is faith.

The same is true of the Trinity. I can understand the concept. I can look at a clover leaf the way St. Patrick used it to demonstrate the concept of the Trinity, but I do not know how or why the Trinity exists and functions as it does.

There are many things that I do not understand, but which I accept. That includes the concept of a soul. I know the soul exists. Because I believe there is an essence of every human being that is much more than the body or the mind. What makes us all do the things we do, where does conscious and consciousness reside? I believe they reside in the soul. The soul is what makes us a person, allows us to communicate and raise our minds and hearts to God in prayer.

And so, it is faith that gives me the ability and strength to accept what I cannot understand. It is that faith that allows me to enjoy the fruits of mankind's ingenuity, and creativity. I love to fly. I love to sail. I love to write. I love to listen to music. I love the sunsets and sunrises. I am thrilled at our ability to launch expeditions into the reaches of space. I love to use the gifts given to me by the Creator to enjoy the fruits of my mind and the minds and souls of others who live now or before me.

I was thrilled when Neil Armstrong stepped out onto the moon. All that because I had faith in our systems that made all that happen.

By the same token, I am thrilled each day at the setting of the sun, and the knowledge that in a few short hours, there will be a brilliant sunrise. The cycle of life will continue. I have faith that that will be so.

WHAT IS TRUTH?

"Honesty is the first chapter in
the Book of Wisdom."
— Thomas Jefferson

We must face the truth. Then we can develop the antidote to the encroachments of age and loneliness. Cheer up, bucko, you are still on the right side of the grass. To stay there, keep fit and never quit.

There is a famous poem "Carry On" by Robert Service from the First World War.

"It's easy to fight when everything's right. And your mad with the thrill and the glory. It's easy to cheer when victory's near, and wallow in fields that are gory. It's a different song when everything's wrong. When you're feeling internally mortal; When it's ten against one, and hope there is none, Buck up, little soldier, and chortle."

"Carry on! Carry on! There isn't much punch in your blow. You are glaring and staring and hitting out blind; You are muddy and bloody, but never you mind. Carry on! Carry on! You haven't the ghost of a show. It's looking like death, but while you've a breath, Carry on, my son! Carry on!"

I have often lectured on the topic of truth and I always began these lectures by asking the members of the audience a simple question "What is truth?"

The replies I get are startling. They span the range from "Whatever Sister tells me," to "Whatever I can prove mathematically."

But the answer I was looking for was something that said that truth is what we determine by ourselves or from external influences, that does not change no matter the circumstances. Truth is what is so, even if we cannot understand it. In other words, truth is truth, no matter the discipline.

Truth is truth. Truth is invariant — no matter what the language, means of description, or medium. For example, if you draw a circle on a sheet of rubber, no matter how you twist or turn or crumple that sheet of rubber, the circle still exists. It never becomes a broken figure, or a rectangle. It is always a closed figure, even if it looks different than the circle. It is still a circle.

Lawyers have a neat way of saying the same thing. Perhaps that is the best concept. They always say, "It is what it is!"

Truth is truth, then, no matter how it is presented or described. It need not be what we see or what we cannot see. Let me give you some examples.

In the desert regions of the world, mirages are common. With the extreme heat, light rays are bent. The image of an oasis miles away can appear before you. It isn't there, even though you can see it. This is called a mirage.

The mirage is a term that could also be applied to relativism. Relativism is the idea that views are relative to differences in perception and consideration. There is no universal, objective truth according to relativism; rather each point of view has its own truth. Perhaps another term could be virtual reality.

For a second example, consider gravity. We can see its effects. We can use it. We can counter its effects and launch rockets. We can even use it to complete flights to the moon. But we don't completely understand it. Nor can we see it. But it is there!

Next time you use your smartphone think of these questions: Why does it work? What is electricity? As you look at the screen, ask yourself, "what is light?"

With all our human ingenuity, experimentation capability, observation, and pondering, however, we still cannot answer all the fundamental human questions about the universe all around us. Or, more importantly, what is life? What is consciousness? What is conscience? What is the soul? What is God?

We can prove the existence of God. We can establish the characteristics of God. We know the history of our relationship with God as recorded in the Bible. Furthermore, we know about Jesus, his life, his death by crucifixion, and his resurrection three days later. We know that the soul distinguishes the personhood of each of us from our bodies and minds. But we still don't know what life is, and other than their spirituality, we don't understand the soul or the nature of the afterlife.

We believe the soul is what distinguishes each of us as persons. We have memory of ourselves at many stages of our lives; and others have their memories of us a well. In a sense, these memories constitute the nature of our lives and they can be construed as our personhood. This characterizes the essence of who and what we are. The same is true for all of us. Perhaps this is some concept of our soul. It directs our actions and it consists at least of our free will, our power of decision, our motivation, and our conscience.

How does this affect our concept of truth? Each of us understands truth from a different perspective.

Consider a sunset. An artist sees a breathtaking array of color and considers the power of God through a glorious display to end the day. A scientist like me realizes the dust in the air disperses the light into the colors of its spectrum, perhaps leading me or scientists like me to comment upon the excessive dust in the air. It is true that the sun is setting. It sets every day. Sometimes there is a magnificent display of color; sometimes clouds obscure everything; sometimes the blinding fireball of the sun just seems to fall past the horizon; but it ultimately becomes dark to signal the end of the day. That is the truth of the sunset, no matter how we describe it.

Equally true is the promise and then the reality of the sunrise. As such, every sunset carries with it the hope of the sunrise. This we know to be true from our knowledge of the truth of science.

Now consider describing a sunset with mathematical equations. This would be unintelligible jargon to the nonscientist. It would be a disaster to an artist who has no scientific training. Yet, the equations describe truth. In the same fashion, the poetic description of a sunset in

Japanese is just as true, but vastly different than the description of a sunset in mathematical terms. Hence, the means by which we describe truth in no way diminishes the fact that something is true. This is an example of the divide between science and theology.

The theologian may shrug and turn away from any type of mathematical or other scientific nomenclature or jargon. The scientist may look askance at logical reasoning to prove a theory that is bereft of equations and experimental results. As the French say, "Chacun a son gout." (To each, his own.)

There is no gulf between the truths of science and the truths of theology. Truth is truth. Any difference in the expression of truth in any discipline is due to jargon and not to the reality of the situation.

I have studied Aristotle, Aquinas, Maritain, and many other philosophers. I have studied relativity and highly advanced mathematics. One subject common to all is cosmology – the study of the earth and its environs in space. These treatises and commentaries all talk about the same thing; but the descriptive language is vastly different. None contradict each other, but there is no agreement on how to describe cosmology. Yet, this is a real science with direct application to our world.

So, there it is. Truth is truth, in all its glory, exactness, and application to our own daily lives, even if we don't understand it, can't see it, or even touch it. Truth does not change. That's life! Great, isn't it?

LOVE – THE ESSENCE
OF HOPE AND CHARITY

"I asked long ago, 'What must I do to be saved?' The
Scripture answered, 'Keep the commandments,
believe, hope, love.' I was early warned against laying,
as the Papists do, too much stress on outward works,
or on a faith without works, which as it does not
include, so it will never lead to true hope or charity."
— John Wesley

As a noun, hope is usually defined as a
specific instance of the general expectation that
something we desire will occur. As a verb hope can
mean to expect or to wish something will occur.
Hope then, is expectation that something will occur.
One example of hope is the desire to be cured of an
illness. We can pray that our illness will be cured,
and it is the essence of hope that the request will be
fulfilled. On a more mundane level, purchasing a
lottery ticket is as an exercise in hope that we will be
fortunate enough to have picked or bought the
winning ticket. Hence hope is not associated only
with religious belief, or with a communication
between ourselves and God, for that is what prayer
is. Prayer is a raising of the mind and heart to be in
communication with God. That communication is
one of thanksgiving or requesting. And when it

19

comes to the requests then it is our hope that that request will be granted.

Why? What makes us think that an all-powerful God, a God that created the Universe, will be interested in granting the wish of a mere mortal? We believe because God loves me and all his creation. It is the belief in love, and the spirit of love, that creates the hope that our requests, or prayers, will be answered.

Our children live in the same hope and expectation that their requests to us will be granted. It is their love which leads to the requests, and our love which leads to the grant of the request. As the song so aptly states, it is love which makes the whole world go 'round.

Charity is a form of expressing love. It is the granting of a gift, even if not asked for, as we seek to spread the Word. Prayer is often performed using intermediaries. We always pray one way or another to God, but we may hope to use an intermediary to add strength and persistence to our request, on the other hand, our prayer is one of thanks giving, then it is direct by us or if it goes through an intermediary then it is enhanced by the strength of our thank you.

It is said that the primary virtues are those of faith hope and charity. Faith as we've already discussed is one factor of our acceptance to what we cannot understand. Hope on the other hand is our relationship with God when our benefits are granted to us and we make requests for new ones.

Charity is a process of giving to others according to our ability to help them. It is our action or series of actions associated with the performance of acts of love directed towards others. It is one way that we exercise the relationship that we have with God where we are created in the image and likeness of God. It is in acts of charity that we actually perform acts similar to those of God.

Faith, hope and charity are the essence of our lives. In faith we accept what we cannot understand; in hope we have an expectation of a benefit that we have asked for; and in charity we have to give to others according to our capability just as we ask God to give to us.

FAKE AND DISTORTED NEWS

"Fake news is a big thing in the field of
Social Media Journalism. Fake news can
be as simple as spreading misinformation or
as dangerous as smearing hateful propaganda."
— Fabrizio Moreira

What if you read a story of a 70-year old man swimming with a tow rope as he towed 70 boats for more than as mile. True or false. In this case, True.

Jack LaLanne was a famous health addict who lived to 96, born in 1914, he died in 2011. Look up his exploits in the web. They seem almost impossible, but they are not. Strange as they seem, impossible to believe, they are all true.

These stories are of interest because they are true, but also because they show what one man can do if he concentrates on the absolute in physical fitness.

It is difficult to always distinguish the truth from barefaced lies. The press today is especially adept at distorting the news for its own purposes.

There are claims and counterclaims that the news is distorted by some media outlets and cases of reporters manufacturing stories that are absolutely untrue. One may think that this occurs with beginner reporters seeking notoriety to achieve rapid promotion. Not necessarily so. Some very famous reporters have been found guilty of deliberate deceitful reporting. Dan Rather, well-known anchor for the CBS evening news for 24 years, was suspended and subsequently left CBS in 2005 after reporting as true a disputed story about President George Bush's service in the National Guard.

Recently, ABC suspended Brian Ross for broadcasting an erroneous report that President Trump was to be questioned by the FBI. This was totally untrue, and some claimed that Mr. Ross knew it.

On November 25, 2016, the New York Times ran the story *Fake News Sausage Factory: This is all about income*. In Tbilisi, capital of the state of Georgia, a former republic of the USSR, a 22-year-old student named Boris earned a living reporting a mixture of real and fake news about Trump or the Clintons. The first story he ever published concerned an incident that never happened. He fabricated a story claiming that Donald Trump slapped a man in the audience for disagreeing with him during a campaign rally in North Carolina.

In Veles, Macedonia, a whole town is set up to generate fake news. Many of the town's digitally literate teenagers are engaged in fake news for export.

There is really nothing new about fake news. The Nazis, with Dr. Joseph Goebbels as their propaganda minister, used this technique effectively for years. The bigger the lie, the greater the chance that it will be believed. Goebbels perpetuated the lie that the Jews had set fire to the Reichstag, the Parliament buildings in Munich, and this monstrous lie was used as justification for the initial repression, arrest, and murder of Jews.

Fake news is being used right now in the United States by the news outlets opposed to President Trump that claim that Russia colluded with the Republican campaign to elect Donald Trump as President. No evidence of this accusation has been found, despite months of searching. Ironically, it has been determined that the Clinton campaign hired a former British Secret Service agent to work with Russian sources to create a report derogatory to Trump. The logic behind fake news is obvious: If the heat is on you, mount a dishonest campaign against the opposition.

The news can also be distorted, even when telling the truth. For example, the following was reported in the New York Times on January 26, 2018:

BREAKING NEWS

Friday, January 26, 2018 8:37 AM EST

The U.S. economy showed continuing resilience in last year's fourth quarter, growing at a 2.6 percent annual rate

> The economy grew at an annual rate of 2.6 percent in the final quarter of 2017, the government reported Friday, finishing off the year on a firm footing — though short of the heady four percent annual growth that President Trump has promised.

Combined with a sinking jobless rate, a surging stock market and a sunny outlook, the estimated overall 2.3 percent rise in the nation's output last year is a sign of the American economy's continuing resilience. The reader's attention is caught. The surge in the economy is important. The Trump administration had indeed indicated that the new tax legislation will spur the economy to 3 to 4% GDP; but the article implies that the President forecast this 4% immediately, and not over the long term. The article also ignored the fact that the economy grew at less than 2% before Trump was elected. Because some of the facts are omitted, the news is distorted, even without fabrication.

Another means of distorting the truth is to be brutally selective in what stories are reported. For example, hundreds of thousands of Pro-Life supporters at the March for Life in January 2018 were addressed by President Trump, the first time a sitting President addressed the marchers in person. Presidents Reagan and Bush addressed them via broadcast from the White House. Fox News and EWTN were the only news outlets to carry the event live and in their news reports.

The next day, the Women's March was covered by all major news outlets. Is this fair? Of course not! Here's the solution:

Speak up with your buying power. Change to a different television and radio station. If an outlet has no viewers or listeners, advertisers will no longer buy air time to sell their products. Then the lying, distorting news outlets will lose their revenue, and they will either mend their ways or go out of business. It's up to you!

STATISTICIANS CAN LIE

"Definition of a Statistician: A man who believes that figures don't lie but admits that under analysis some of them won't stand up either."
— Evan Esar

Don't be a statistic, whether true or not. Lead your own life. Pick your goals, pick your methods, and go for it!

Statistics may be an exact science; but the people who manipulate the statistics can produce lies.

For example, let us say a statistician is concerned with establishing the likelihood that electric cars will be purchased by the general public. Instead of asking the direct question, "would you buy an electric car?" a statistician who wants a certain answer would first describe its short range and the cost of a battery charge. Currently, it costs $15-$17 to recharge an electric car battery. The normal range of a charge, depending the car, can be less than 100 miles or as much as 600 miles. By and large, however, the cost of powering the car with electricity is greater than fueling it with gasoline. So, after first explaining this to prospective buyers, then asking "would you buy an electric car?" the result of the survey would certainly be skewed by people realizing that the cost of powering an electric car would be greater than powering a gasoline-combustion car. The pollster never mentioned that the cost of maintaining an electric car is significantly less than gasoline engine. Hence, the results of the survey would be skewed to the negative.

In the same way, if interested in doing a poll on the approval rating for the president, the statistician hoping for a certain answer could ask "Do you approve of the president's handling of the immigration issue?" or "Do you approve of the president's handling of the North Korea issue?" Because these are controversial subjects, those who approve of the president in general may not approve of his decisions regarding immigration or North Korea. Therefore, the range of approval would be a scatter, with those who approve of the president overall showing up at the low end. Hence, the statistician could produce a report saying, "Approval rating for the president is low" when, in fact, it may be very high, but the approval for specific issues may be low.

Statistical surveys, then, depend on the way the questions are framed. It would be impossible to manipulate the numbers of the analysis, since these are scientifically sound. So, beware. When you see surveys, try to find out the exact questions that were asked.

Another critical factor in statistical polls is the selection of the respondents. For example, some of the most interesting surveys that were incorrect were those associated with the presidential election of 2016. Most surveys indicated that Hillary Clinton would win the election, yet Donald Trump became president. Even if the correct question is asked, it is impossible to survey the entire population, so a small sample is selected. The typical sample is 1,000 to 2,000 people. If you want to skew the results, then make sure you pick people whose answer you know will be on the side that you favor.

Hence, statistical surveys can be skewed by manipulating the questions to be asked and/or by controlling the selection of the people to be asked. A so called "impartial" survey can thus be very partial.

One could say that statistics are correct, but that statisticians lie. Judge for yourself.

This is especially true of statistics for people my age and yours.

SOLVE THE RIGHT PROBLEM

"If you're in government, the right thing to do is be focused on solving real problems and asking what's the best solution to a particular problem."
— Julius Genachowski

I am still alive, and so are you. I intend staying alive. Do you? I never quit. Do you? I will not let the calendar kill me. So, I have to solve the problem of defeating the grim reaper.

That's easy!

To stay alive, be alive! That's the problem to solve.

It is surprising how often people run helter-skelter to solve a problem when the problem they are trying to solve is the wrong one. This came to my attention when I was working with the U.S. Army on various special projects. I bumped into a Major who told me an amusing story about how so many young officers don't know how to give the right command. He described the following problem given to the officers as an assignment in command school: "You are in command of an engineering company under heavy fire. The task is to build a bridge across a river. What is the first command that you, the commander of the company, should issue?"

33

The Major then went on to tell me that rarely does anyone get the right answer. The correct answer is "Sergeant, get that bridge built!" The reason this is the correct answer is because one attends command school in order to learn how to give commands!

I am reminded of some hilarious and some not so hilarious but wasteful instances during my own career, where the wrong problem was being solved.

One of the funniest was at a major plant of a pharmaceutical company. As I walked in, I saw a ball, about five feet in diameter, hanging from the ceiling of the factory, dripping water. I couldn't help asking my guide, "What is that?" The guide kindly explained that it was part of the process of making toothpaste to which I quizzically responded, "What?" The guide went on to explain that toothpaste is made by adding pumice and flavoring to liquid milk of magnesia and then draining off the water. I burst out laughing. I just couldn't help myself. After I got myself under control, I said to the guide "Why don't you just take magnesium sulfate, add some pumice, some flavoring, a little water, then stir, and that's it?"

So, you see, the correct problem to solve is how to make toothpaste economically and based on a modern technique. The wrong problem is how to make toothpaste based on an 1850's technique!

I also did some consulting for a smelting company that wanted to build a soaking furnace at a cost of some hundred million dollars. The company already had two soaking furnaces. Soaking furnaces heat large ingots, or blocks of metal, so they can then be rolled. Each soaking furnace had a capacity of holding four ingots; but the average was only three ingots of the same alloy. The proposal was to build a third soaking furnace in order to increase production because of the incomplete capacity of the existing units. Even though I was aware that the soaking times, or heating, for each alloy were all different, I just asked one question: "What happens if you heat an ingot for longer than it is necessary?" The reply was "Nothing." So I said, "Then why don't you put four ingots in every soaking furnace, no matter the ingot type alloy?" The answer was "We never thought of that!" So, they were solving the wrong problem— a hundred million dollars' worth of a wrong problem!

One time, I visited a paper rolling and cutting operation. The paper rollers were something like 132 inches wide and were rather expensive. The waste can amount to something like $250,000 per inch/year. Of course, the goal was to have as little waste as possible. The normal practice was to use the same width; so that if they desired a 12-inch roll they would set the machine up to divide the 132 inches into 12-inch rolls. But if they had an order for 10-inch rolls, there would be a certain length of two-inch-wide waste. So, I asked "Why can't you mix and match the various desired widths of paper so that you can fill up the entire length of the roll?" The reply was: We never thought of that!" Once again, what problem were they solving?

And now one final example. I was asked by the general manager of a metal factory how to produce more of a particular alloy because it had the highest profit margin. I studied the situation and found that the optimum product mix was to not produce his high margin alloy at all, because it was also a hog in terms of the time required in the plant. Well, this led to a heated argument until I proved it to him mathematically. After that, he became a strong advocate of a procedure called optimum product mix. It's one of the very first operations research mathematical solutions devised. That which appears to be obvious is often incorrect. Solve the right problem. In this case, the right problem was how to increase the profitability of the entire plant, not just the profitability of a single product.

I am by nature, a systems engineer, if not by training. All my professional life I have been concerned with systems of one kind or another. In systems engineering, as in computer science, as in rocket engineering, the basic rules of the game are:

Define the RIGHT problem.

Solve THAT problem.

Implement the solution.

Measure the real impact of the solution against the desired solution.

Modify the solution to meet desired impact and cycle again.

So, there it is. Unless you solve the RIGHT problem, you are wasting time and money.

And remember, when making your toothpaste, use magnesium sulfate rather than milk of magnesia, and then treat the family to dinner with the money you save!

For guys and gals my age, the right problem to solve is staying alive. That means to live. Walk on the grass.

COMMON CORE

"Common Core is a big win for education."
— Bill Gates

Remember what it was like in school! In the days before the twenty-first century, chewing gum was the worst thing you could do. While school was tough for us, it was the learning that we had trouble with. Now learning is a secondary thing. Now the teachers might be assaulted. Teachers are happy to survive each session. What a terrible change that will affect all of us for years to come.

We have been too easy on our kids. We want them to have a better life and better schools than we had. But what is the reality? Our public schools have become a problem rather than a solution.

Hopefully Common Core will solve some of the problems we face in our public schools. Our schools are too important to ignore.

We face a serious problem, if not a crisis, in our public educational system in the United States. Despite many excellent public schools around the country, numerous statistical studies point to a decline in achievement averages versus those of private schools, church-related schools, chartered schools, and schools in other countries.

One attempt to remedy this situation is a set of educational achievement goals called "Common Core," currently in Mathematics and in English Language Arts, for all levels K through 12. The goal of Common Core is to institute consistent educational standards nationwide and ensure that students graduating from high school are prepared to either go to college or to enter the workforce. This program has created an unintended stir. It was designed to set standards and minimum targets of achievement that would be better than the average today, and consistent with educational standards in other countries. It has stirred controversy because it has achieved mixed results; in some cases, it has resulted in lower achievement levels than hoped for. Why?

Consider the manner of education today. A group of students are addressed by a single teacher, occasionally assisted by another instructor. The ratio of students to teachers is kept quite low. The desired ratio is 15:1, but it is typically 20:1, or more. The range of aptitudes and abilities of the students varies as widely as any cross section of the population. In any group of 20, how many are really paying attention? How many have the mental capability to grasp the material? And how many are even interested in learning? In such an atmosphere, to whom does the teacher aim the instruction? If aimed at the highest level of intelligence and interest, more than three quarters of the class will be left behind. If the lessons are aimed at the lowest level, a different group of students will be bored and turned off. So, the teacher will aim at the center of the group, thus incapacitating the lowest level, and boring to distraction the gifted. By setting a common level of instruction, by necessity, this has aimed the instruction level at the midpoint of all students.

The counter to this is to establish classes with different levels of ability. This is somewhat undemocratic but is done to satisfy the needs of different levels of the students. But then again, this was always so. The concept of "fast track" or "scholarship level" has always been a factor in education. The danger is that Common Core will eliminate that approach and seek a common level of understanding and education that is below the highest and above the lowest.

Since its inception in 2010, the pace of implementation has varied widely from state to state and district to district. The results have been just as varied. In some districts, there is an apparent improvement. In others, no improvement, and in some, a lowering of standards. There seems to be no consensus on the value of Common Core. Some states have taken steps to improve the situation. Other states have abandoned the concept.

Truthfully, no solution has been found that will solve the falling achievement levels in our schools, public or otherwise.

Let me suggest an alternative. For centuries the forum of education was the Socratic method, where a single teacher was surrounded by a small group of students all discussing the material to be learned. The students would enter the forum having already read the material and would be prepared to discuss at length the fine points and application of the material. This method of instruction was actually used by Socrates, hence, the name.

We will never have a Socrates available in every classroom in the country. But we could use robots.

Teaching robots could teach the fundamentals to individual students at their own pace. Gifted students would be encouraged to pursue additional subjects to enhance and enrich their education. Hence, the gifted would be challenged and average students will be able to absorb the minimum required to advance to the next grade. All non-tracked students could meet daily to reinforce the subject material and discuss how it will be useful in their lives. This exchange will be of great benefit to all students who have learned the fundamentals of the required subjects. In addition, the gifted students would meet separately with teachers trained to supplement their course work with more advanced subject matter and possibly pursue additional subject matter. This would most likely be language arts and other branches of history or science.

An educational system that incorporates robots could meet the needs of all students and would most certainly result in higher levels of achievement than the methods in use today. In addition, it would eventually lower the annual cost of education per student.

How practical is this concept? In fact, this approach is being followed now across the country with the wide use of computers, laptops, and tablets in the classroom. The success of such instruction can also be gauged from the use of these techniques in college-level programs. There are some universities, most notably Phoenix, that are based heavily on remote learning with mechanical devices. This approach at least deserves to be tested in the real world of the classroom.

It is essential that we do something about our country's low achievement levels in international testing. Education of our children is too important not to receive the priority it deserves. We need a core achievement system. It can be done by thinking and working "outside the box."

LIBRARIES

"Libraries allow children to ask questions about the world and find the answers. And the wonderful thing is that once a child learns to use a library, the doors to learning are always open."
— Laura Bush

We need libraries. That's where our children really grew up, searching and finding the world of yesterday and today and tomorrow. The use of tablets and smart phones at the dinner table is no substitute for real libraries.

I have been in many different libraries during my lifetime. There is some thought that libraries will eventually become extinct in this digital age where books can be downloaded electronically, or people can even download audio books which means you don't have to read at all.

I, however, do not believe libraries will become extinct. There are many people like me that go to libraries for the sheer peace and quiet. Besides, they have now become much more than a repository of books. If nothing else, there are computers connected to the internet for patrons to use. In addition, you can borrow audio books, videos, and even old fashioned 8 mm movies. My library at my summer home has Tai Chi classes. Libraries have become polling centers for local, state, and federal elections, information centers for news and local events, and I am certain they will begin serving fast food. They have become gathering places for local citizens as well as places to borrow books.

When I was a young boy of around eight or nine, it would take me 25 minutes to walk to our local library in Toronto, just a little bit farther than the grade school I attended. Until I was 12, I always entered through the youth entrance. There were all kinds of attractive books to read: Doctor Doolittle, The Swiss family Robinson, Robinson Crusoe, the books of Robert Lewis Stevenson, and many humorous anthologies of which I no longer remember the titles. I enjoyed my trips to the library. Once I got there, I felt so at home among the other young people, all sitting at long tables and reading.

There wasn't a lot to do during the thirties. There was no television — just one radio per household if you were fortunate. We did have a Victrola and my father had a collection of 78-rpm records which he had collected over the years. I used to love to play them. Two songs I remembered vividly from those days are "Red Sails in the Sunset" and "Smiling." But no one had any money. Even going to the movies for a nickel wasn't always possible. We didn't realize that without money we were supposed to be miserable. We were too busy having fun to realize we had no money. We weren't poor. My father had a job. We just didn't have any money; so, we made our own fun and we were certainly happy in our environment. The library was free, and it was an outlet for me.

Beginning at age12, I was allowed into the adult section of the library. What a new world! I began reading books on submarines, air battles, anthologies from World War I, and of course, books on science. The books I really enjoyed were those of Roy Chapman Andrews, the archeologist who discovered dinosaur eggs and traveled throughout China. To say the least, I was a veracious reader. I had read an article on speed reading and followed the rules so that by the time I was 14 I had established an ability to read quite fast.

When I went to the University of Toronto, I discovered the stacks in the student library. I went down into its bowels and found books that had been written a couple centuries ago. I was studying mathematics and physics at the time and it was fascinating to sit and read my way through the original texts of such giants as Newton, Lagrange, Euler, Einstein, and so on.

Years later, I was fortunate to sit on the board of the Gregorian University Foundation. This took me to Rome where I discovered the Vatican libraries. There I poured over the tomes of some of the most illustrious figures in history: Galileo, Aquinas, and Descartes, for example. Some were pretty dusty but thrilling to see and use. Then I happened to be in Jerusalem and visited the Jesuit Biblical Institute, where I was ecstatic to handle papyrus scrolls dating back to the fifth century. It was as if I were there with the authors at the writing of these historic documents and I am so grateful to the libraries that house and preserve them.

Libraries are the repository of the ideas, beliefs, and works of the greatest minds that ever lived. For me, these minds come alive again in a library and share their thoughts with me. "Ah," you may scoff and say: "A digital image is just as real as a musty, dusty, scroll of parchment." Perhaps. But not all old papyrus scrolls have been digitized. Even if they were, they could never give the reader the same sense of timelessness and intellectual connection with the authors.

The present-day electronic search engines are very useful, and fast, but there is no guarantee that the information is correct. The only way to be sure is to dig deeply into the electronic references. My approach is to check a fact I really know is true. If the reference is different, I discard it as questionable.

Libraries which offer the "real" thing, then, are often the final resort to truth.

A library is a place of calm, a place where you can commune, albeit only one way, with some of the greatest minds that ever lived. Where else can you sense that you are talking to someone who lived two thousand years ago? Visiting a library can be quieting, it can be exhilarating, and it can be challenging. My hope is that these human cerebral assemblies of the centuries never die!

WRITING

"Either write something worth reading
or do something worth writing."
— Benjamin Franklin

Writing now creates the historical documents that future generations will use to write the history of these times. You didn't know you were so important. Without your writings and mine, history will have a hard time. You didn't know you were so important for the future generations of humanity. So go for it! Write! Tell the story of these days for all the future generations.

I always wanted to write. I find it easy and I enjoy it. Even though I was studying science, mathematics, space flight, and the like, I would have preferred to have majored in English and History and spend my life as a professor of English. Instead, I became a Professor and department head of Systems Engineering at the University of Waterloo because I also like to solve problems and build systems. Yet, I still wrote many books and articles.

My first publication, at age 15, won third place in a contest on Economic Factors in Unemployment During the Great Depression. I submitted the paper and was absolutely startled and elated beyond belief when a check for $15 dollars came in the mail for third prize. That was not a trifling sum in 1945.

In high school, I used to write essays on various subjects that caught my attention. I remember I wrote one on the differences between the military tactics of the Romans with their Legions and the Persians with their Phalanxes.

Somewhere around age 16 or 17, I read that if you wanted to write, you should write every day. I bore that in mind when I got to the university, and I began writing for *The Varsity*, the University of Toronto daily, which had a circulation, at that time, of about 20,000. I think we were the third largest daily in the province of Ontario. I wrote feature articles for *The Varsity*, conducted interviews, and I even contributed to writing a humor piece. The discipline of daily writing is really the key to successfully develop writing skills.

To date, I have written 28 nonfiction books and five novels, and one radio play. I wrote the radio play my first year of graduate school, after I met Fr. Daniel A. Lord. He had come to Toronto to produce the play *Every Nun*, commemorating the 100th anniversary of the arrival of the Sisters of St Joseph in Toronto. I attended most of the rehearsals and got to know Father Lord rather well by spending many evenings kibitzing with him in the back of the theater. After rehearsal, he would sit at the piano and play ditties and sing with everybody for ten to fifteen minutes before breaking it up for the night. He became everybody's friend. Of course, he would. He was a Jesuit!

Writing is supposedly a lonely art. It is, if you're writing nonfiction, but not when writing fiction. In all my novels, I entered the scene and became the protagonist. When I wrote the book *The Resurrection — a Criminal Investigation*, I became the Roman general, or tribune, Quintus, sent to Judea by the Emperor Tiberius to investigate some nonsense about a criminal who had supposedly risen from the dead. I spoke to the apostles Peter and Paul, Mary, Jesus of Nazareth's mother, and I actually felt like I was directing the investigation. The only time I had difficulty being Quintus was during the meetings with Tiberius. I tried to portray Tiberius as a fair emperor, but he was really a scoundrel. I also participated as Quintus in the meetings with Pontius Pilate. There are various images and concepts of Pontius Pilate portrayed in history, but in my opinion, he was extremely weak and cruel. He could not govern and was a disgrace to the Roman concept of governance. One of the best scenes of all my writing is the last meeting between Quintus and Pontius Pilate, when Quintus pounds his fist on the table and shouts at him "Govern! You are a Roman. Govern!" I think that says it all.

I have written twenty-three technical and religious nonfiction books, five novels, and a three-volume autobiography. The first volume of the autobiography is titled *Stories for My Grandchildren* and covers my youth through graduating from university. The second volume is called *Scientist and Writer* and covers both my careers. The third volume is titled *Changing the World*, because I did. I invented the smartphone. I also invented some other things that I wrote about in that volume. I knew I would be changing the world dramatically with the invention of the smartphone because I was putting the entire world at the fingertips of any user, anywhere. You had to be naive not to realize how that would revolutionize the world. I just couldn't understand the indifference and subsequent delays because people could not fathom the device's capabilities until it was sitting in the palms of their hands. Only then did they know.

I almost did it. I was only defeated when a world class chip manufacturer falsified the specs of the chips they supplied my company. It became impossible to use the smartphone as a phone and computer at the same time with that chip. That caused a three-year delay. By that time, I had run out of money and was not able to borrow anymore. I had to stand by and watch all the large companies start building smartphones, infringing my patents at will. When confronted, they responded "Sue me." So, I did. I sued the entire industry. I sued 169 companies. 101 settled, but 68 went to the Obama administration and were able to change the law. That I could not fight.

So first I changed the world. Then I wrote about it.

Why do I write so much? Why do I write technical books? Because I am basically a teacher. I like to be able to impact young minds, in particular. I loved being a professor at the University of Waterloo, Ontario, and at NYU. I taught graduate students at Waterloo. I still remember the seminars I conducted there. My Ph.D. candidates weren't much younger than I. We would have a game of touch rugby and then go in and have the seminar. One day, I twisted my back and I laid down on the table in the front of the room and gave the seminar from there. There was a mutual respect, and I think affection between myself and the students. They have all gone on to remarkable careers. I am gratified that I had some part in moving them toward that success.

And how do I write? I write the way I speak. So, I sit and talk to my reader, explaining very complex problems in engineering, mathematics, and science. You may not like to read my books, but then again you might. They are well read and seem to have a good following. Let this series of essays be an introduction to the way I write.

READING IN THE 21ST CENTURY

"You don't have to burn books to destroy a culture.
Just get people to stop reading them."
— Ray Bradbury

If nobody reads nobody knows what happened in the past so they must relive it. Read and create. Read and bypass the mistakes of the past. Skip reading and stagnate. Besides, it's fun.

I read a recent piece concerning John Lukacs, Professor Emeritus of History at Chestnut Hill College in Philadelphia, who taught courses that my wife Barbara attended. A photo showed John, surrounded by books, somewhat distraught that people were no longer reading books. It seems that there are many counter currents to acquiring information or entertaining oneself other than by reading books.

Books are wonderful. They contain the distilled thoughts of writers, whether they are dissertations on authors' philosophies, or manifestations of their imaginations in short stories, novels, or poems. In the past, books were read for either entertainment or for the acquisition of knowledge. Let's examine both of these in turn.

The many forms of entertainment today are almost overwhelming. Any sport, drama series, or comedic presentation may be watched on TV or downloaded and streamed on a computer, smartphone, or tablet. Even a myriad of concerts can be attended without going to the concert hall and sitting in an uncomfortable chair. There is just so much that can be effortlessly consumed for entertainment purposes these days, that reading a book and using one's imagination is just too much work.

What's more, everyone is a critic. Anyone who has a device and access to the Internet can comment on anything and anyone, without fully knowing the subject about which they are judging.

As far as the acquisition of knowledge, any specific question can be asked, and the response downloaded onto a smartphone, tablet, or PC. There is no limit to the topics that can be studied. It is all at your fingertips, and available immediately on many different forms of media.

Why walk or drive to a library and borrow a book that you must return, when you can have it all on your smartphone? Maybe it would be worth the trip.

We have no time for books. We have instant news and instant reaction to the news, with very little expression of thoughts in a coherent and cohesive presentation. Since very little thinking is happening, we can be manipulated, and we are vulnerable to mob mentality. Yet, one hopes that the decency of the human spirit will prevail.

What about tweets? They can be offensive, devastating, interesting, humorous, or inspirational. Most of us know that the President tweets; so does the Pope. They both also have their speeches and sermons broadcast via radio or television. The objective is mass communication of their specific messages for specific occasions. There is nothing wrong with using the media for mass communication, whether in short bursts or tweets, or in longer messages via television or radio. Influential men are sharing their messages and their views with the people they serve.

And isn't that what the Gutenberg press was intended to do during the Renaissance in the 15th and 16th centuries? The objective was to take the place of the scribes and monks by mass producing valuable manuscripts to reach far beyond the distance that the human voice could travel. When Jesus preached the Sermon on the Mount and gave us the Beatitudes, it was only possible for those close by to hear him. If Jesus where here today, he could broadcast his message to the entire world via television, radio, or the Internet.

In *Understanding Media: The Extensions of Man,* Marshall McLuhan said the medium is the message, and that we live in a global village. This will be especially true with the satellite linkages expected in the next two years which will provide instant global communication to everyone on earth.

Will the reading of books increase or decrease? It will probably decrease, and that is tragic, but reading will probably increase. After all, if you read enough tweets, or enough material from an internet, then your reading will probably increase. You may read more in small bursts than you would while reading a book. No longer will we curl up in a soft chair for an afternoon of reading what some brilliant mind wrote a few thousand, a hundred, or even ten years ago. We will no longer take the time to absorb someone's creative imagination in a quiet relaxing atmosphere. Instead, we will frantically pour over text on some screen, hungry for more, and more, and more. Reading will no longer be a luxurious way to spend an afternoon, or evening, or that blessed hour in a warm bed before falling asleep.

So welcome to the world of reading, 21st century-style, as opposed to reading in the 16th century, or even in the twentieth. I am resigned to reading less from a book than from a screen; but I resist it as far as I can. Ooops! There goes my tweet button. Gotta run!

COURTESY

"Who does not prefer civility to barbarism?"
— C.S. Lewis, *The Four Loves*

Me!

Let's be civil. It can be uplifting.

Men in the past might have been quite flowery in their words and actions. Big sweeping gestures as they removed their hats and bowed to the ladies. We usually don't even wear hats today. Do we have to stop the flowery greetings?

Maybe we should go back to wearing hats, and to sweeping them off, and bowing as we greet someone with a heartfelt "Good Day!":

Sounds like fun. Good exercise too!

Civility is a noun that essentially means showing respect for another person's words, actions, beliefs, and demeanor. We all have many images of civil behavior. Perhaps the most common historic memory of civility is that of Sir Walter Raleigh removing his cloak and spreading it over a puddle to prevent a companion's feet from getting wet. We have been told that in the past, civility was commonplace in our U.S. Congress, with flowery language and wide sweeping gestures showing respect for the opinions of others.

Today, we are overwhelmed with video images of people shouting at each other, trying hard to keep the other person from being heard. Sometimes, even facial expressions can be uncivil and more disruptive than shouting matches. The classic example was perhaps the Vice-Presidential debate of 2012, when the Vice President was on camera grimacing and contorting his face disdainfully, punctuating the statements of his opponent. Another way to show contempt for our neighbors is to talk down to them, belittling their words with technical jargon or sarcasm.

The rapid spread of technology has left millions in its wake feeling inadequate and incompetent, as they try to cope with the tsunami of change. It was Albert Einstein who stated, "It has become appallingly obvious that our technology has exceeded our humanity." This is even truer in today's cyber age.

So how does one cope with the breakdown of civil behavior in our streets, in our government, and in our board rooms and on the world wide web? How do we train children to be civil when so many stars in the sports, entertainment, and business world are uncivil boors, trampling over rules of decent behavior, often with impunity? "In your face" confrontation seems to be the norm of the day. Do we follow the path of the least common denominator of society, and follow the "leader?" Where are the heroes for our children to emulate? How do we ourselves hope to behave?

Think again! Maybe it is not as bad as it seems. As former Secretary of State, Condoleezza Rice said: "I don't believe in confrontation. That seems to me outside civil discourse and we all have to find ways to be civil to one another." That's the key. We *must* find a way.

It was William Penn who alluded to it many years ago when he stated: "I know no religion that destroys courtesy, civility, and kindness."

It seems that the breakdown of civility has coincided with the rise of secularism. The religious mandates to "love God above all else, to "love your neighbor as yourself," and to "turn the other cheek" are all but forgotten as we love ourselves above all else and seek to attack and excoriate our neighbor.

It's easy to be kind. We should all try it. It doesn't hurt. It might even be contagious. There is a famous Spanish fable of a dour disfigured man who donned the mask of a happy-go-lucky youth. Years later when he died, the mask was removed and lo and behold, his disfigurement was gone, and his face had become that of the mask.

Remember that song of our youth. "Put on a happy face." Fake it, if you must, but do it!

FIRE IN THE BELLY

"Someday, after mastering the winds, the
waves, the tides and gravity, we shall
harness for God the energies of love,
and then, for a second time in the history of
the world, man will have discovered fire."
— Pierre Teilhard de Chardin

At one time in my younger years I was a Professor of Systems Engineering at the University of Waterloo. My students were a mixture. I could spot the ones that were going to go on and be successful, and those that were questionable. The difference I detected was what I came to call "fire in the belly". Some students who were athletes and who were always stars on their team, seemed to have a go, go, go spirit. They were the stars of the team and of the league. In the classroom, there were some students who had the same spirit and drive, and some did not. Those with the go, go, go spirit were the leaders. I found the same spirit and distinction in the world at large. The difference was fire in the belly – the drive to succeed.

This distinction was certainly evident when I lectured overseas. The students in Asia, especially in Singapore, Taipei, and Hong Kong, all had fire in the belly. They wanted to succeed. They often spoke of companies they would form, and not necessarily jobs they would have. The drive was to create. Nothing would stop them. To some extent I found the same thing in American and Canadian Universities. It seemed that the more financially comfortable the students were, the less intense the fire in the belly.

Mine was always intense.

I was born in 1929 and grew up during the depression years of the 1930's. Nobody had any money, but nobody was poor. My father had a job, so we definitely were better than poor, but we still had no money. Nobody had any money. So that was no downer. But we all had fire in the belly. We were all determined to get past that part of history and to work our way upward.

I had a summer job by the time I entered high school. I also had a weekend job. There was no disgrace in having a job like that. Many of my friends delivered papers in the morning. I found it more convenient not to deliver papers getting up at five or six in the morning, but to work on weekends and during summers.

Despite a heavy work load we had lots of fun. We spent weekends on the beach because my hometown, Toronto, was located on Lake Ontario. We would take a street car down to the docks, hop on a ferry boat, and within less than an hour from the time we left home, we were on the beach. This was certainly cheaper than hopping on a plane to some Caribbean island. As a matter of fact, we didn't even think of that. Passenger transport by air was just coming into its own in the 30's and didn't become popular until the 50's. In any event, every weekend we had a family gathering somewhere, during a summer on the beach or on somebody's farm. It was a joyous occasion.

But we all talked of things we were going to do. We had ambition, we had desire, and we had fire in the belly.

As I look back on all the cousins and friends who used to gather on weekends like that, there have been some remarkable success stories. Of the cousins, we had five MD's, two lawyers, one PhD besides myself, two dentists, and one psychologist. It was quite a gathering. Of the MD's one became a department head at the university as well as practicing quite effectively in bacteriology.

We all had fire in the belly.

TECHNOLOGY IS RUINING MY LIFE

"We live in a society exquisitely dependent on science and technology, in which hardly anyone knows anything about science and technology."
— Carl Sagan

I don't have a moment's peace. No matter where I go, I get text messages, email, phone calls, or other plain and simple disruptions to my life. Just imagine what it would be like without technology. We would have silence. We wouldn't have our blaring TVs, noisy cars and motorcycles, or constant dings as our cellphones alert us to a message, email, or phone call. Give me the old-fashioned days where all you would hear was the clippety-clop of the horses shod hooves on the cobble stones, although you may not enjoy the smell of manure as it hit the ground. But there weren't that many horses, so the streets would have been mainly silent. Wouldn't it be great to have lived back then?

Are you kidding? With all those diseases, short life spans, tedious travel, continual wars, poverty, and wild economic swings. Skip the past and push for a bright future. The good old days were not so good.

Of course, you might not have lived as long since the lifespan was a little shorter in those days. I think it was somewhere around age 48; while today we are living into our 80s. But at least life was enjoyable when we weren't so distracted by noise and continual new inventions. Just think of life before the invention of the smartphone. You might leisurely walk to the library which may have been four or five miles away. Then you could spend the entire day going through a whole series of book to find some fact or reference that you were looking for. Sometimes you couldn't find it in that library, so you might have to walk another ten or fifteen miles to another library and sift through another set of books. But at least it would be quiet. You wouldn't have the constant buzz of intercoms or the stupidity of people pulling out their smartphones and doing a Google search, with the tap tap tap on the screen, or the smartphone providing audible answers to the user.

And then, wouldn't life also be a little bit quieter when you traveled? The only thing you'd hear would be the rumble of the stagecoach wheels and the clippety-clop of the horses' hooves, and perhaps every once in a while, just that special whiff. Wouldn't that be a lot better than the noise of a jet and sitting in an airbus, being propelled at enormous speeds across the planet, occasionally bouncing erratically after bumping into some turbulent air, disrupting your peace of mind, as you wonder if you're going to stay in the air, hit the ground, or ultimately arrive at your destination?

Ah, the good ole' days. I think I'll definitely give up my smartphone and stop traveling by jet.

I may have to cheat a little bit because taking a stagecoach to the other side of the country might be a little cumbersome. Maybe I can settle for just using a propeller-driven airplane. There are still a lot of DC3s in operation. It wouldn't be too bad because a DC3 will take me across the country in maybe two or three days. At least I wouldn't be flying 35,000/40,000 feet buffeted by the jet stream. I could fly leisurely around 2000 to 3000 feet, granted I will be tossed about by thermals rising from the ground, or the various storms as they occur.

While I'm at it, I'll give up my car and you give up your car and let's get rid of all cars, at least until the electric car has mastered noiselessness and the gasoline driven monster that we call a modern automobile becomes obsolete. In the meantime, get yourself a horse and buggy. Or better still, if you have a family, get yourself a covered wagon to replace your SUV. I think they used to sell them on Conestoga Road. I live close to Conestoga Road, so

I'll look up and down Conestoga Road to see if I can find somebody who makes covered wagons.

Ah, for the simpler life. No more jets, no more cars, no more cellphones, no more text messages, no more Google.

Just imagine. People will have to talk to each other instead of texting as they walk down the street side by side. What will it be like without text messages? You won't know what is going on. You won't get tweets or even snapchats. You won't get email either, but you don't read them anyway.

I'm going to begin a new organization dedicated to returning to the old days. I think a good name would be BBOD – Bring Back the Old Days. I used to belong to an organization called The Independent Order of Old Bastards. I was only in my 40s then. Now in my 80s, I wouldn't dream of belonging to such a reactionary bunch of old geezers.

I want you to think about organizing a BBOD movement in your community. Let's all go home and throw away our smartphones, or better still, burn them. We'll synchronize our sundials, get some combustible material, wet the phones with a hose, and then then set them on fire. This will create a lot of smoke. Then we can start sending smoke signals. However, keep semaphore flags handy just in case your cellphone doesn't make enough smoke. Either way, we can send messages without having to use smartphones. You might even contact some of your friends by smoke signal or semaphore and ask then to set up relay stations. Pretty soon, we'll be able to go intercontinental with our messages.

Hmm. Sounds like a good idea. Might even by grounds for an IPO that will make me a billionaire.

Fellow thinkers, you are leaders of your communities. Be leaders in the new BBOD movement. Get rid of your smartphones. Start sending smoke signals.

THE TECHNOLOGY TSUNAMI

"Learning how to understand how technology evolves, using tools like a Technology Road Map, is what you need more than anything to ride on top of the tsunami instead of being crushed by it."
— Peter Diamandis

This is a "Wow! Factor" in living today. Be a part of the "Wow! Movement." Push it. Get others to use it. This is a great time to be alive. Aren't smart phones better than smoke signals.

This is a unique time in human history as far as technology is concerned. Of course, we have had technological developments throughout history; for example, the discovery of fire, the invention of writing, the invention of the wheel, the printing press, the airplane, the computer, and so on. But today we are on the brink of an exponential burst of technological breakthroughs into our daily lives as never before. It is a veritable technology tsunami.

What are these technologies? They are varied between hardware, software, and what Dr. John Mauchly[*] and I have always termed "brainware".

---

[*]John Mauchly designed the first general purpose electronic digital computer.

Here are a few innovations that will be making their debut very soon.

3D printing has been around since 1983, but now we have arrived at the stage where we can use 3D printing to create prototypes for body parts, musical instruments — we are limited only by our imaginations. It is even being used to design prototypes for houses. There's no end in sight to the range of applications of 3D printing. At this time, 650 square foot houses are being built at a cost of $4,000. This is a straw in the wind.

Quantum computing will revolutionize our ability to handle very complex calculations or to sort through vast reams of data in just a few seconds. Quantum computing is based on the ability to have multiple states in a quantum array. For instance, using "X" as an example of quantum states, we can see how we can create computers millions of times faster than what exist today. Until now, all computers have been based on the binary system, one or two, for a yes or a no, a high or a low voltage. We have used this system to create today's ultrafast capabilities, up to millions of calculations per second. With quantum computing, we can multiply that by thousands or millions, as we have at the designer's disposal, "X" states to select almost infinite combinations of yes or no. Just think of the combinations that you can arrive at even with an array of "X" states, leading to an almost infinite set of possibilities.

We have not ignored the problem of data storage. Years ago, while solving an online storage issue for a client, my company determined the need to erect a three-story building to house all the data units. Now we can store the same amount of data with a single handheld device. We have developed the ability to compress storage down to one terabyte onto something the size of a postage stamp. With today's technology, we are storing so much information that we are considering storage farms in the Arctic or at sea because of the heat. Quantum computers will render the data storage problem obsolete.

Soon solar panels will supply much of the planet's power because they have developed to the point that one kilowatt hour can be produced for just pennies. Think of the impact of clean solar energy in the city, in the factory, and in the home. And what about during the night and inclement weather? Batteries will soon take care of that.

Battery technology has now been developed so that we can put a battery in a car and give it significant range and speed characteristics. Our smart-homes can also be powered by batteries, if necessary, and even entire cities, soon to be powered by solar panels, can be powered by batteries during darkness or inclement weather. Excess stored energy will charge batteries which will release power whenever necessary. Sounds like science fiction, doesn't it?

Then there are the computer chips that process all the information these newer technologies will use in smart-homes, smart-speakers, smartphones, and just think...smart-clothes! You will be able to go out into the coldest winter weather and your smart-shirt will react to the cold, close up the tiny spaces in the fabric of your shirt, keep you insulated from the cold, and perhaps turn on a battery in your back pocket to keep you warm. Your shirt may also be made from cloth woven with nanobodies and nanotubes.

These are only some of the technologies that are ready to burst upon our daily lives. What will they do for us? They will generate a virtual reality or augmented reality that will allow us to walk, for example, through a home or office before it's built, or to visualize anything that we are dreaming about creating. Augmented reality will allow us to meet with people who are scattered around the world as if they are in the same room with us. Think of that. Family gatherings every night, no matter where we are on the planet.

Finally, artificial intelligence, or AI, will bridge the divide between today's devices and applications and the imminent technology tsunami.

Lest you be fooled, artificial intelligence is *not* intelligent; hence, the adjective "artificial." It is an expert system, designed by a human programmer to solve a problem. A human programmer conceives all possible outcomes of a certain action, and then establishes the conditions required for those outcomes to occur. The learning capability of computers is also a misnomer. Computers only make use of the data preprogrammed by a human being. There is no learning whatsoever by the machine. The learning comes from setting the conditions required for some action. Those can be "learned". The use of Decision Tables can facilitate this "learning". This is very powerful.

Artificial though it may be, AI will become common place in our smart-homes and in the robots that will one day populate every one of those homes. Robots will be an important element in our daily lives, especially when it comes to taking care of the elderly, in particular those who are suffering from mental or physical disabilities. Robots will be in every home, every schoolroom, and every work place.

You will no longer go to the hospital, but a medical system will come to your home or wherever you may be. Robots will also be employed to farm on the tops of high rise buildings in cities with a significant reduction in the cost of food, and they will take on all dangerous jobs such as fighting fires, mining, and offshore drilling. But offshore drilling may even be a thing of the past as the entire petroleum industry changes dramatically because of solar energy, which will power the electric car.

The cost of living will drop dramatically, but incomes may also fall as millions of jobs are displaced by the robots. Governments all over the world are already examining the concept of a guaranteed annual wage for all citizens. Life will never be the same again. It will proceed at a different pace with more time for leisurely activities.

There is a danger, however, associated with the fact that everyone in the world will be connected. This could very well lead to a need for greater security, which means an increase in our nation's defense capabilities. Yet, despite all the mechanical, technical, economic, and security issues that will undoubtedly arise, I believe we can look upon the technology tsunami as something that will lead to the Second Renaissance of the human race on planet Earth. Exciting, isn't it!

NOTE: For a fuller description and outline of all the effects of *The Coming Technology Tsunami,* see my book of the same title.

A MEA CULPA FOR THE HAVOC
AND PROMISE OF TECHNOLOGY

"New technologies are wreaking havoc on employment figures – from EZ passes ousting toll collectors to Google-controlled self-driving automobiles rendering taxicab drivers obsolete."
— Douglas Rushkoff

This new world will never make me obsolete. But I apologize for making many people and industries obsolete. The buggy whip and smoke signals were obsolete before I came along. So were typewriters and telegrams in my time. Now many more things are obsolete. But there are some good points. They far outweigh the bad. Think a bit. In the meantime, please accept my apology for disrupting your life. Ha!

I'd like to say a few words — three in fact — about my new book. Some of you may think it's about my old book, *The Coming Technology Tsunami* but that's my old book. The new one is called *Apologia pro mea curiositos* (Apology for my curiosity). And here are the three words: I am sorry! I apologize for the terrible harm my curiosity has inflicted on humanity.

First: My curiosity has created addicts out of all your children who use smartphones. They cannot live without them. They cannot have a meal without their smartphones by their sides. Thank goodness their teachers are smart enough to prohibit smartphones from coming into the classroom. Personally, I would like to have them prohibited from church as well as from coming to dinner. But then again, my own smartphone is right next to my plate, just like yours, and we are both often interrupted by messages and urgent emails we must read and answer. So, let's be very careful about banning our children from bringing smartphones to the table, lest we realize we need that discipline, ourselves.

Second: I apologize for the fact that my invention has destroyed conversation. You and I have often seen young people, walking down the street texting each other, rather than talking. Believe it or not, they also sit side by side in one of their living rooms, texting each other, rather than chatting. For this, I abjectly ask your pardon. On bended knee, I ask your forgiveness.

Third: I beg your pardon for the fact that I have destroyed your health as well as that of your children. You once walked five miles to the library (if you couldn't get a ride) when you had to look something up. Now, you merely text it into your smartphone and allow Google to do the work for you. So, Google is very healthy, and you are rapidly becoming a couch potato. I am also sorry that your children no longer turn to you with their curious questions because they also turn to Google. That is a precious loss.

Fourth: I must apologize because the index fingers on our children and ourselves are becoming ossified and pointed to better manipulate the touch screen.

Fifth: I must also apologize for the fact that your right arm, if you're right handed, or your left arm, if you are left-handed, has permanently elongated so that you can hold your cellphone in that hand while you take selfies. I am also sorry for the artificial grin forever planted on your face so that you are always ready for a selfie.

Yes, all of this requires your pardon. But wait. There's more. Shall I get on my knees now? In 1952, purely by chance, I discovered something called plasma in shockwaves. At that time, I suggested to some German rocket scientists that instead of building a 65-story tower, filling it with explosives and lighting a match, it might be more elegant to have a rocket ship first take off like an airplane, then accelerate into outer space using first turbo jets, then ram jets, and then plasma propulsion.

The Germans told me in no uncertain terms that I was a child and I didn't know what I was talking about. I was twenty-three years old.

But it is on the verge of happening. There is currently extensive research regarding plasma propulsion for extraterrestrial rocketry. Excursions to the moon and eventually Mars will most certainly use plasma instead of rocket fuel.

The next ten years are going to be dramatic as I've discussed in my old book *The Coming Technology Tsunami: A Personal History of the Future*. In the United States, every home will have a robot. We might even have a robot run for president. As I write, there is an effort in New Zealand to build a robot meant to run for political office.

Somewhere in the next two to three years, a series of satellites will be launched so that everyone in the world will be connected. Can you imagine the disruptions when messages come from any part of the world any hour of the day or night? And we were concerned about the dinner table!

It is going to happen. The Second Renaissance is upon us and — please forgive me — there is no stopping it. So, I ask that you pardon my curiosity and hence, the creation of the smartphone and my contributions to space flight.

And for those of you who cannot forgive me, I have agreed to begin a new organization dedicated to returning to the old days, i.e., snail mail and smoke signals, foot-travel, and horse-drawn buggies with free manure for the flower beds — all you can use. The club's first requirement will be the relinquishing of your smartphone. Ready to sign up?

ARTIFICIAL INTELLIGENCE ISN'T

"By far, the greatest danger of Artificial
Intelligence is that people conclude too
early that they understand it."
— Eliezer Yudkowsky

Or perhaps that they cannot. You will not be able to duck the impact of AI on your future. So, join it. It is easy enough to understand. If you can do it, you can get a machine to do it. It is that simple. It might be a little difficult, at times, to program a machine, but at least the concept and theory will be definable, and quite probably understandable. The best approach is just to dive in.

The press is full of stories about the dangers of artificial intelligence (AI). When will it take over? How long before it outsmarts us? The press concentrates on the negative and describes the hazards, which may or may not exist. But the hazards are certain to occur and are right around the corner — at least as far as the press is concerned.

The term "artificial intelligence" is a misnomer. There is no "intelligence" in artificial intelligence. A more appropriate term might be "expert systems."

An expert system, or AI, is something that we already know how to do. We conceive of all the possible outcomes of a certain action, and then establish the conditions required for those outcomes to occur. For example, consider running for political office in the United States at the federal level. This means running for congress, running for the senate, or running for the president. The requirements to run for congress are to be a resident of the state, to be 25 years old, and have been an American citizen for at least seven years. The requirements to run for the senate are to be 30 years old, a resident of the state, and an American citizen for at least nine years. The requirements to run for president are to be a natural born citizen of the United States, a U.S. resident for 14 years, and to be at least 35 years old. These conditions are laid down in the constitution and any situation outside these conditions rules out a prospective candidacy.

So, AI can be quickly established by asking the pertinent questions for the citizenship, birth, resident, and age requirements. This can be set-up in a truth table, or Decision Table; and, in turn, can lead to setting up a computer program to test the validity of a candidate for federal office in the United States.

Perhaps a more interesting example of artificial intelligence would be planning a trip to someone's house in another city, considering all the ways of traveling to that location, including flying, taking a train, or driving. In each case, there would be several combinations of possible routes. All potential routes would be selected by a computer system dedicated to establishing the route for the trip. After establishing certain boundary conditions, such as the mode of transportation, the starting point and destination are entered into the computer, and the AI determines the number of possible routes. The AI could pick the fastest, most inexpensive, the most scenic, the least congested or, if driving, one that includes a place you'd like to visit. Taking all conditions into account, the expert or AI system would generate an optimum path to meet all your conditions.

So, you set out on your trip and there's an unforeseen problem such as heavy construction on a highway or a closed airport, for example. The AI system could immediately generate a new optimum route dependent on the revised conditions you enter into the system.

There is no way the AI system can know what you are thinking, therefore only you can determine the boundary conditions, that will impose restrictions upon the AI system.

To assume that the AI system would be able to generate the boundary conditions based on your past experience would be a stretch. With the history of all your previous trips to the same destination in the system, the AI would be able to select and present the most frequent. However, if the most frequent of your trips always included the fastest and most economic, these conditions could be selected, based not upon an intuitive or selective process, but rather by a historical set of preferences preselected by you. If there were no pattern to your trips in the past, then the AI system would ask for your boundary conditions before presenting a solution.

I think you can see quite readily that there is no intelligence in AI whatsoever. Checking according to a predetermined set of commands, executing according to boundary conditions, or asking for boundary conditions when none exist can be done by AI, but only because all the possible results are preprogrammed into the system.

There is no doubt that AI will become a very important element in all future devices and systems that the human mind is creating and is destined to create. But there will never be a robot or computer program that will be able think, create other systems, create other robots, or take over the world. That is the realm of science fiction.

Driverless cars are a form of AI. While reading about how they operate, I discovered that the analysis of motion was foundational to the programming. So, if a driverless car is following another car, and that car comes to a stop, then the AI program will stop the driverless car as well. But if the car being followed pulls into another lane, and there is a stalled object in the path of the driverless car, then the driverless car will plow right into the stalled object. Not very intelligent, is it? Perhaps the AI programmer should have had written it so that the driverless car would stop when it detects an object ahead, no matter what it is. I suspect that correction is being made.

DON'T FEAR THE SECOND RENAISSANCE

"Change creates fear, and technology creates
change. Sadly, most people don't behave
very well when they are afraid."
— Daniel H. Wilson

Are you going to be a positive factor or a dormant slug during this Second Renaissance? Will you help create it? Delay it? Skip it? Or best of all, help create it, move it forward, and enjoy it?

Technology has been a tremendous benefit throughout history, but is often feared, ridiculed, and opposed. One of the greatest examples in history is the reaction to the Gutenberg Press in the 15th century. It was termed the "devil's device," and even led to riots throughout Europe. Yet, when you look at it dispassionately, the only people it affected adversely were the scribes who were copying books and other literary works by hand. The Gutenberg Press produced books by machine and set into motion a revolution for products of the human mind. The Gutenberg Press was the father of the Renaissance of the fifteenth and sixteenth centuries.

Technology has advanced dramatically since the Gutenberg Press to affect our daily lives forever and is much more than electronic gadgets, driverless cars, and robots. Advances in chemistry, physics, biology, farming, transportation, communication, education, and political systems are also technological and they are not always in such esoteric areas; but are also seeping into the mundane parts of daily life such as our supermarkets. Consider, for example, Walmart and Amazon. It is a different world entirely.

Technology is any new development involving the making, modification, usage, and knowledge of tools, machines, techniques, crafts, systems, and methods of organization in order to solve a problem or to perform a specific function. It is based on a new set of ideas and techniques, and usually incorporates more than redirected human labor.

Our standard and manner of living have changed dramatically since the 15th century. Today we have antibiotics instead of blood-letting; we have jet flight instead of horse and cart; we have instant worldwide communication with satellites, the internet, and smartphones as opposed to hand written documents that could take weeks or months to arrive. These are only some of the changes that technology has brought us in a relatively short period of time. It has been just over 70 years since the first digital computer was demonstrated publicly on February 14,1946. That machine occupied 1,000 square feet and was comprised of 18,000 glass vacuum tubes, not all of which worked continuously, or together. In the words of the co-inventor, Dr. John Mauchly, it was "the biggest test-tube rack in the world." The smartphone, which can be held in one hand, and can be dropped on the floor and immersed in water and still function, has over a million times the capacity and speed of that machine.

There are over four billion smartphones in the world today. It is the ubiquitous means of communication, entertainment, and employment for billions of people, from toddlers to centenarians. The smartphone has changed the world and the world is in the hands of its user. With this device, you can see and be seen, hear and be heard, and exchange ideas, smiles, jokes, and tears with anyone, anywhere, anytime. It has finally made the mantra of Marshal McLuhan come true. The world is indeed a "global village" and soon the whole world will be connected!

During the past ten years, there has been a certain global repression in the application of new product lines, and generally in the enhancement of business. There has been pent up demand, but at the same time, there have been remarkable developments in research. The results of these developments are about to explode with a host of new capabilities, products, and procedures that will dramatically affect the lives of everyone on the planet.

In less than two years, everyone on the planet will have access to the Internet via satellite networks that will make it possible for everyone on the Earth to communicate with each other. Currently, over three billion of the over seven billion inhabitants of the Earth are connected. Imagine the impact when that number more than doubles! This will create huge demands for products and services all over the world, not just in the so called "developed world."

Modern satellites are very small, weighing less than 10 kilograms. They can be launched in clusters, which significantly reduces the cost of shooting them into orbit. The dollar savings will make it possible for industry, rather than government, to launch satellites networks. It is conceivable that even small companies will be able to launch their own satellites.

Communication capability will increase, and the cost of such communication will decrease. Such communication will not only be much cheaper, but also much more secure. The day of the "hacker" will soon be over.

With each innovation in technology, there are those poised to take advantage of it and use it for destructive purposes. Hacking is a serious problem and often makes the headlines. Currently, the number of attempts is estimated to be in the hundreds of thousands per month. However, the cyber-attacks that make the news are more likely cases of error, poor security procedures, and/or copying passwords. Most of the successful attacks are the result of electronic devices, or "backdoors" imbedded in a computer that enable a hacker to take control of the system and download or change the data, at will. Hacking in the form of trial and error to duplicate a password is in the realm of science fiction. It rarely succeeds. Properly created passwords, with strings of unrelated characters, of a significant length, over which security measures are kept and maintained to avoid discovery, cannot be penetrated or copied or found. Computers may be used to generate possible password sequences, but this would require millions of attempts to log in, which is impossible if a system is properly designed. Properly designed systems allow no more than three password attempts. If not successful, the machine locks for twenty-four hours.

Most of us remember the highly placed government official whose password was the word "password." Well..., at least he had one. Many people ignore the gravity of password security. Some often have no password or stick it with a post-it note to the face of the computer. Some forty to fifty years ago, while creating systems for electronic wire transfers, I recommended strict control over access to computers that sent electronic instructions to move money — up to three trillion dollars a day. We often installed the computers in cages with strict control over who had authority to enter. None of these systems were ever penetrated.

When I say the day of the hacker is finished, I mean that it is now possible to discover "backdoors" implanted in the hardware. Processes are now available to detect hacking. These processes initiate a series of programs that would locate the hacker and take counter measures that may be disastrous for the perpetrator. Such counter measures can even lead to the destruction of the hacker's computer and/or networks.

What are some of the other advances in technology that will impact everyday life in the next five to ten years?

Most dramatic of all is the potential cure for cancer. Instead of chemotherapy, doctors use agents that stimulate the immune system to kill the cancer. This is currently affective with cancers such as lymphoma, prostate, some brain, and blood cancers.

It is expected that soon immunotherapy will also cure lung, breast, bladder, and various other cancers.

Perhaps the hottest topic of the day is artificial intelligence — the driving force behind robots, driverless cars, teaching machines, and remote diagnostic systems. Artificial intelligence and artificial learning systems are misnomers. There's no such thing as an intelligent machine. Humans examine processes and procedures and determine in minute detail how these processes and procedures really function. Then they are programmed into a computer. In other words, artificial intelligence is really nothing more than an expert system, designed by a human, which performs a function according to rules created by a human, and installed in a computer program. Self-modification of the program is not a case of the machine learning; rather, the human designer has predetermined all possible outcomes or steps to be performed by the computer program. Can all the possible outcomes be determined? Yes, based on all possible conditions for testing that can be established. It may not be known for certain what an outcome may be, but with the foreknowledge that it exists, observation and experiment can discover it.

For example, in the late 1920s, astronomical observations indicated the existence of a large body at the extreme end of the solar system. Further examination revealed the large mass, eventually called Pluto. Although once considered a planet, Pluto was downgraded to a dwarf planet in 2007. If we know it is there, we can go out and find it.

Again, there is nothing artificial or intelligent about this "machine learning." The detailed examinations of all possible alternatives, performed by humans, are programmed into the computer. All actions must be established, or they cannot be programmed. The computer then follows a specific path once certain conditions occur. The effect can be startling at times, but remember, no machine can ever be imbued with the intelligence of a human being. Machines slavishly follow program conditions that are laid down by a human programmer.

One of the great advances of the next decade will be in personal medicine and remote medicine. The location of the emergency room, to a large extent, will be wherever you are. The doctor will be on call and you will be in video communication with that doctor, no matter where he or she is. That may seem far-fetched, but such capabilities were demonstrated as far back as the 1980s.

The driverless electric car is also here. While much of its projected use is based upon it entering streams of traffic anywhere, I believe that roadways will be modified to create lanes for self-driving cars, like bicycle lanes. In addition, personal car ownership may become rare. "Uber"-like systems, with or without driverless cars, may soon replace the use of personal vehicles. At the very least, small cars for local transport and large cars for long distance may become the norm.

One of the most interesting advances that will become commonplace in the next ten years is augmented reality. Virtual reality, or the ability of a computer to generate the ability to walk through a house that doesn't exist, or to use a machine which doesn't exist, has been around for some time. Augmented reality will create the ability to appear to be in a meeting room as if you are present, appearing to be sitting at a conference table, talking to your colleagues as if they are seated there with you. Each participant could be in a different part of the world. Mind boggling, isn't it? But nice!

The advances in technology over the next ten years will explode like a tsunami. The impact on the world will be profound. We will have robots in every home and we will talk to them. They will be able to provide education and training, so that more time will be spent on the application of technique, rather than on learning the technique.

New jobs will be created by the millions, but technology will also wipe jobs out by the millions. This will create hardships for those who do not have the skills required by the new technologies, but these skills can be learned, relatively inexpensively, likely through machines. Hence, it will depend on the will of the individual as to how he or she will cope with the inevitable changes in our lives due to technology.

Just think of the impact in the undeveloped world with the tsunami of technology making a whole new set of capabilities possible.

I predict that this technology tsunami will go down in history as a Second Renaissance. In the first Renaissance, art and pursuits of the mind became not only possible, but accessible to ordinary people. The same will occur in the 21st century. I also believe the importance of faith and family will be reborn and there will be a greater emphasis on the human spirit, i.e., the nature of the soul. I believe faith will become increasingly important as people have more time for leisure and to examine various aspects of morality, and to easily exchange ideas and opinions with others anywhere in the world, at any time.

Technology should not be ridiculed, condemned, or feared. Technology is really the

106

result of the human mind examining who are we, what are we, and how we are. We have always wondered about the universe around us. Technology just makes it easier. Perhaps we can finally determine the nature of gravity, although we already know how to use it.

Use technology. Do not be afraid of it. Do not condemn it. Do not avoid it. Do not ignore it!

As a human being, I am excited at the prospects of what technology will create for humanity in the next ten years. As a scientist, I will seek to make it happen. Together, we can change the world.

I hope you too are excited; and will do your utmost to bring about the Second Renaissance.

THE PROBLEM OF GOD

"Most people really have no problem with the idea of a creator God. Their question is just what is this God like, how can I know about him, how can I know him?"
— Eric Metaxas

God is a mystery?! We can prove that God exists, but it is difficult to rationalize our relationship with God. The most famous depiction of God is on the ceiling of the Sistine Chapel. There the image of God is that of a benevolent bearded man whose finger is giving life to an inanimate Adam.

Tradition has it that we are made in the image and likeness of God. We tend to think of that image as being one of human appearing characteristics. On the other hand, our sprit and our souls might be made in the image and likeness of God. That presents an entirely different concept.

So, let's take first things first. How do we prove the existence of God?

We just have to look around us.

As a scientist I can look beyond what I see in my immediate vicinity, and I can look at the entire universe. It is remarkable! What a wonderful creation. It stretches 40 million light years. It is still expanding. And it is still hurtling through space. We live in an expanding universe that is gigantic in size. That universe did not come by chance. It did not spring into existence on its own. There was a creator. That creator we can think of as God.

From a scientific point of view if we can think of God as a quasi-infinite, if not an infinite energy field. That infinite energy field created the mass that exists with all of the stars and planets in all of the universe. The conversion is according to the relativity equation $E=MC^2$. Only a quasi-infinite energy field would be sufficiently large enough to create the mass of the universe. Since the universe exists, then the infinite source of energy from which the universe was created must exist. That was God.

As they say, the proof that God exists is easy. What is not so easy is to begin looking at the attributes of this God.

We think of God in a highly personal fashion, thinking of ourselves having a one to one relationship with God. That may very well be so. A God that is infinitely powerful to have created this universe certainly can have one to one relationship with billions of people at the same time. How is that done? I don't know. But the God that created this

Universe can certainly have the power to be in a one-to-one relationship with everyone for all time. This is the spiritual nature of God.

God, then, is a spirit. That spirit can connect on a one-to-one basis with our spirit- or our soul. Our soul permeates our entire being. We are mind, body and soul. We can, and are, in communion with God. The vehicle is undoubtedly our guardian angel. But with our infinite God, that connection can be direct, as well as through intermediaries, such as the Blessed Virgin, the spirits of our relatives, and the spirit of the saints, and our guardian angels. Our direct relationship with God can also be directed to anyone of the persons of the Trinity. That is an even greater mystery. Many of us have felt the presence of the Holy Spirit in our lives. That is the true essence of God- the spirit. And so, I wonder, who am I? What am I? Why am I?

Even more so in the prayer of the Holy Spirit:

Come Holy Spirit, fill the hearts of your faithful and kindle in them the fire of your love. Send forth your spirit and they shall be created. And you shall renew the face of the earth.

O, God, who by the light of the Holy Spirit, did instruct the hearts of the faithful, grant that by the same Holy Spirit we may be truly wise and ever enjoy His consolations, through Christ Our Lord, Amen.

Why did God create us? Out of love. Every indication that we have of communication from God is the message that says, "Live and be happy." God wants us to be happy.

To ensure that happiness and to give us assistance, we believe that God has given each of us a Guardian Angel. It is the Guardian Angel that could very well be the instrument of the one-to-one relationship between us and God.

We can communicate with our Guardian Angel. We can often feel the presence of this spirit at our sides, guiding and counseling everything we do. As I child I said that prayer which I still remember so vividly:

> <u>Prayer to My Guardian Angel</u>
> Angel of God, my guardian dear,
> To whom God's love commits me here,
> Ever this day be at my side
> To light and guard,
> To rule and guide. *Amen.*

I often wonder if my Guardian Angel is my mother, still looking after that little boy she left behind when he was eight. I often felt her presence, especially at exam time. I almost saw her at the

corner of the desk smiling and feeding me answers
to the tough questions. That says it all, doesn't it?

IS FAITH NECESSARY IN
THE CYBER AGE?

"Human behavior is more influenced by things
outside of us than inside. The 'situation' is the
external environment. The inner environment is
genes, moral history, religious training."
— Philip Zimbardo

Faith in God might be considered passé in our
current cyber age. Some agree with Karl Marx and
look upon religion as an opiate for the people,
something to assuage fear of the unknown, or a set
of superstitions not based on reality or solid
scientific facts. Today, when we reach for the outer
edges of the universe with our telescopes and rocket
ships, we sense the power of our intellects and the
extent of our accomplishments. We humans have
moved from exploring the caves where we lived to
exploring outer space in a just few thousand years.
Religious shackles can be thrown off as we flex our
minds and muscles, especially now with the aid of
the computer which has enhanced our mental
capability. And yet, as we discover more about
ourselves and the universe, we come up with even
more questions as to who we are, what we are, and
why we are.

What are your questions? More importantly, what are your answers? Why do you live? What is life? Why were you set to live now? What will you make of your life? Who have you helped? Why?

We all have brains that direct the activities of our physical bodies, store our memories, and somehow direct our thinking and consciousness. But what is consciousness and what is the process of thinking? How do we formulate the words that express an idea? How do we create music? How did Einstein come up with the theory of relativity? How did Michelangelo conceive the design for the Sistine Chapel? In short, how do we think? "Ay, there's the rub," Shakespeare so eloquently expressed in *Hamlet*.

Stop for a moment and ponder this seemingly simple question. Then take the question a step further, doesn't the reality of human thought also imply the existence of free will? Without free will, we would not be able to choose yes or no, right or wrong, and many of the great philosophic propositions accepted today would never have been possible.

The ability to think and the manner in which we think makes us unique. This is the difference between humans and animals. Lions, for example, can think, but do not possess the ability to reason that is unique to human beings. If they did, they would likely come together and take over the world. This is probably true for all animals.

Only humans possess intellect and free will to choose a best course of action. Such a course of action may contradict the gnawing in the pit of a human's stomach when the brain signals that it's time to eat. But would a lion stop a feeding session to admire a beautiful sunset? Probably not. Would you?

So, what has this to do with religion in the cyber age? Simple. The more sophisticated our study of the universe becomes, the more we realize it could not have come from nothing and we move closer to a belief in a creator. While the universe and all the creatures in it may have evolved over time, there was still a point from which it began. Even the atheist admits the "Big Bang" theory is the explanation for how the universe began. But how did that mass that expanded, and is still expanding, come to be? Where did it come from? Scientifically, we know energy creates mass and energy is created from mass, but neither is created from nothing. So how did the mass or energy at the instant of the Big Bang come to be there? Again, we can use the Hamlet refrain – so faith is necessary, perhaps even more so, in the Cyber Age. In fact, we probably have more faith in more things than any of our ancestors. "Ay, there's the rub." So, even in this technologically advanced cyber age, we find more and more that faith in a creator is not an opiate, but a reality.

IS THE INTERNET REALLY INTERFERING WITH OUR YOUTH GOING TO CHURCH?

"Turn off your email; turn off your phone; disconnect from the Internet; figure out a way to set limits so you can concentrate when you need to and disengage when you need to. Technology is a good servant but a bad master."
— Gretchen Rubin

Getting young people to go to church was never easy. Bright summer days, fishing, biking, or almost anything was always an excuse for not going to church services. Now it is the internet that is blamed. In reality it is just the nature of the problem.

So, solve the right problem. Make it interesting so young people, and old people, want to go to church services. Make it interesting. Make it desirable. Make it useful.

Technology seems to get blamed for everything. A recent piece in "Aleteia" (an online publication which offers a Christian vision of the world by providing general and religious content that is free from ideological influences) concerned a survey that indicated that our youth were not going to Mass because of the internet. The statistical survey seemed authentic, with the results skewed towards the excuse that the internet and their busy lives prevented young people from going to Church Services.

I disagree. I think the reason young people do not attend Mass is because they did not get adequate training in their faith and therefore have no real appreciation of the Mass.

There are a number of reasons for this. First and foremost, they probably had a religion teacher, if they had religious training at all, whose training was also not deeply rooted in the knowledge of our faith. Those from my generation were fortunate to have consecrated brothers and sisters teach us religion while we were in school. Whether in a CCD program or in Catholic school, it was the sisters who ground the tenants of our faith into us.

In the fall of 2014, I began meeting in Philadelphia with Charlie McKinney, president of Sophia Institute, now a part of EWTN. He spoke of his concern over the quality of the religious education in the elementary and high schools in various dioceses around the country. Charlie gleaned firsthand knowledge as he traveled around the country interviewing people about books they were writing or trying to publish. He explained that the Sophia Institute was going to develop a series of lesson plans for religious education teachers throughout the country, but he also emphasized the necessity to develop orientation programs for the teachers, so that they would become aware of the advantage of these lessons plans and how they could enhance their own knowledge of the faith, as well as enhance their ability to teach it. He had already received a positive response from the Diocese of Los Angeles. They hosted their first workshop in August of 2014 and then ran five programs back to back in the diocese of New York. Now Charlie was talking to me about Philadelphia. I contacted a great friend, Barbara Henkels, a major benefactor to Catholic education in Philadelphia. Barbara has done a tremendous service to Catholic youth in the Philadelphia area with her brainchild, the Regina Academies, educational institutions dedicated to the classical approach to Catholic education. Now, there are five Regina Academies in Philadelphia, thanks to Barbara and her late husband Paul M. Henkels.

Barbara was very enthusiastic and between the two of us we funded the Sophia Institute's program in Philadelphia. Barbara funded the elementary schools and I funded high schools. The first program in Philadelphia was in the spring of 2015. In Charlie's words "once those three large dioceses were 'knocked down,' it just grew exponentially. Some of the most respected superintendents allowed us to train their teachers."

Recently, I received an email from Charlie which said, "Less than four years ago, we set out to transform Catholic schools into our best centers of catechetical and spiritual formation. Forty months later there are 39 dioceses that host the Sophia teacher training workshops. 13,252 teachers are being trained, 22,301 students are being formed through the new K-8 textbook series, and 29,243 teachers receive the Sophia Institute's weekly email lessons and activities."

This success was beyond our imaginations when we first began; but it can be done. It takes an idea and the determination to see it through. I share this hopeful story because there is a tendency today to shrug our shoulders and feel hopeless when we see so much nonsense going on all around us.

You see, the internet cannot be directly blamed for young people not going to Mass, and with the Sophia Institute's program, our youth can begin to realize they receive more from the Mass than they give by simply showing up. The Mass gives them the grace and fortitude to withstand the secular assaults upon their faith that they surely encounter on the internet.

Often in life, we try to solve the wrong problem. We pay attention to one thing, then realize it wasn't the problem at all. For example, as I began this essay, I wrote about the internet being the reason why young people don't go to Mass. Then I described the true problem — deficiencies in Catholic religious education across the country.

So, when you discover a problem tugging at your heart strings, first pray, then speak up, define the problem, be persistent, and do something about it! And God bless you!

MAKE A MESS

"By keeping your eye on the ultimate goal,
you lean into the mess and try to make
the outcome a little better."
— Jeff Fortenberry

This is a phrase attributed to Pope Francis. It is a perfect example of the difference in idiomatic expressions in different languages. The Pope's intention was to get people involved. For him, "make a mess" meant to get involved. A more idiomatic translation might be "stir the pot". So... are you stirring the pot in your life.

I was walking my dog around the neighborhood when I bumped into my skeptical friend George. Before I could even say "Hi," he jabbed his finger in my face and jeered, "That Pope of yours must be crazy. He told those kids in Rio to 'make a mess.' What kind of nonsense is that?"

For a moment, I was speechless. The Pope's message — a very important message — was lost on George. "George," I began, "you misunderstand. The Pope wants the young people to challenge the status quo, even if they mess up. He told them that making mistakes is part of growing up, of being human. If you do nothing, of course, you won't make mistakes — so one may think. The Pope is saying that doing nothing is a mistake. He urged them to act; and if they err, they should seek forgiveness and move on. He is challenging them to get involved."

"Humph," George spluttered. "What's wrong with the status quo? Everything is fine and dandy. We don't need a bunch of kids upsetting the apple cart. The Pope should tell them to be quiet and just listen to those older and wiser than themselves. Just like we did."

"George," I said, "If we keep the status quo, there won't be any progress. We wouldn't have any jet planes, space travel, television, computers, or cell phones. There is a famous story about the superintendent of the US Patent Office, at the turn of the 20th century, who stated how chagrined he was that everything had been invented, and nothing new would be possible. That, of course, was before the vast explosion of technology up to the present."

"So what!" interjected George. "Kids didn't do it."

I couldn't help laughing. "George, tell that to Bill Gates, Mark Zuckerberg, Steve Wozniak, and, if he were alive, Steve Jobs. They were 'kids' who made a mess."

"Humph," George answered. "You have a point, but only a point. The status quo is normally fine. The stock market is a perfect example. Stocks like stability."

I chuckled again. "George," I said, "you're mixing apples and oranges. The markets like stability because then they don't have to work at finding good investments. As much as they like stability, they like new companies and new products even more. Companies like Apple, Cisco, and Facebook became the true darlings of the investment community. Progress changes the face of everything. We cannot remain stagnant. Dying industries will do anything to inhibit progress. Just think of buggy whip manufacturers. They strongly opposed motor cars because they put an end to buggies and buggy whips. Surely, propeller manufacturers opposed jet airplanes. Thomas Edison faced tremendous opposition to electric street lighting by gas companies who supplied gas for street lights in New York City. I could go on and on George. The biggest proponents of the status quo are the executives of the companies that will be affected by change. It has always been so, George."

George was silent, and his face became very thoughtful. "So that's what the Pope meant," he said.

"Yes. He wants the young people to step up and be heard in the affairs of the church. Just as he wants greater participation by the laity in church matters."

"But that can't be," George said. "The laity, and especially young people, are not trained in theology and scriptures. How can they become involved in matters of the Church if they are not trained?"

"George, you're both right and wrong. Think about it. A man goes to the seminary because of a vocation and is ordained after years of training in theology, philosophy, the scriptures, and the magisterium of the Church. He does not get an MBA in Finance or Administration along the way. He might do that later, but certainly not as part of his seminary training. Besides, that is not his vocation. His vocation is spiritual, not temporal."

George was nodding his head. "So, what does the Pope want?"

I sighed. "George, the Pope is asking for our help and prayers. The Church is comprised of the laity as well as those who've chosen religious vocations. All must be actively involved. There is a role for everyone. The days of a division between the religious and the laity are over. We are all human. We all make mistakes. We all sin. Love is what binds us all together as we follow Jesus. What we believe doesn't change; but how we act in that belief can change. It's all right to make mistakes. We all do. We have to forgive and move on. So that's why the Pope told the young people to 'make a mess.' He actually told the whole Church the same thing."

George nodded, but remained silent. My words had affected him. Perhaps he now understood the danger of blind adherence to the status quo.

My dog began tugging on the leash, so I said goodbye to George and walked away. I left George standing on the corner deep in thought. Maybe he'll decide to "make a mess."

POLITICALLY CORRECT

"Being politically correct means saying
what's polite rather than what's accurate.
I like to be accurate."
— Robert Kiyosaki

It's strange that people often would rather be politically correct than factually correct. This book is not politically correct, but hopefully it will be correct for your future. Do what is right. State your mind. But be factual; and be right. Saying the wrong thing may be political but not correct.

In order to be "politically correct," or "PC," you should not use any phrase or behave in a way that may offend a particular group of people, e.g., a political party, religious group, social movement, etc. For example, a Moslem may find a cross or crucifix offensive, so Christians should refrain from wearing them in front of Moslems. By the same token, Christians may find Moslems turning to Mecca in prayer five times a day offensive, so Moslems should refrain from doing so in front of Christians. Unfortunately, in the United States these days, it would be politically incorrect for Christians to express their preferences or beliefs in either scenario above. This is because in the United States, being PC implies that you do not offend political parties, religious groups, social movements, or any particular group of people endorsed by political parties.

The claim that you must always be in line with the platform, practices, and beliefs of the democratic party in order to be politically correct is ridiculous. This term, until recently, had nothing to do with the democratic party. It meant that the beliefs, opinions, or customs of one group are not favored over another. If something is truly politically correct, it is neutral. If it is neutral, then there is no bias on the side of any party. Otherwise it is CP — completely prejudiced.

Nowhere is this prejudice more evident than on college campuses. These bastions of free speech believe in free speech for one side only. If the campus leans to the left, then they deny the right of a conservative to speak. Any means of suppression, from catcalls to violence, is PC.

One egregious example that comes to mind is the claim that religious symbols are offensive. The claimant may be one out of a hundred thousand people, yet, since that person claims that it is not politically correct to display the religious symbol, that person is heard. This one opinion or claim often affects the whole population. Can you imagine attending a wedding where one person is offended by the figures on the top of the wedding cake or by the ceremony of marriage itself? What a way for a guest to behave. Bad manners to say the least.

There are, unfortunately, too many instances where the media is prejudiced to the left or to the right. A reporter may not necessarily lie but omitting facts favorable to one side or the other is just as irresponsible as direct outright fabrication. In a sense, omission is a very effective form of lying. Too many of the press reports in the mainstream newspapers today are prejudiced. Why can't the media go back to the "old days," present the facts and let us make up our own minds? The misrepresentations are tiresome. Personally, I have reached the stage of questioning the veracity of whatever I read, no matter which way the journalist leans — left or right.

What's the point of fabrication, omission, or deliberate twisting of the facts to give advantage to the prejudice of the journalist? Why bother? If something is so blatantly prejudiced and omits facts which can be ascertained otherwise, then the reader will rapidly become aware of this — that is to the say if the reader wants to know the truth. The reader may very well be aware that the journalist is prejudiced toward a certain viewpoint, and for that reason, is following that particular journalist. But if your mind is already made up, then why bother reading anything?

I must say that as I get older I am becoming more and more impatient when I read a story that is obviously falsified, distorted, full of omissions, and written by a journalist who has no interest in providing the facts. I become impatient when it is shoved at me as if I am too stupid or indolent to gather the facts and make up my own mind.

Hence, I think that the current concept of "political correctness" is incomplete, it is politically corrupt, and politely contemptuous — contemptuous of the reader, that is. I hope that you will join me in trying to eliminate it so that we can go back to the old-fashioned news stories that carried the facts without editorial twisting and turning, leaving you and me to make up our own minds.

Let's have a return to civility, a return to free speech for everybody, a return to tolerance for the opinions and beliefs of everyone. If we do, then we can hope that henceforth PC will stand for politely correct!

SHOOTINGS

"I don't think there should be more gun control. I
think there should be more education."
— Sam Brownback

Shootings are the great tragedy of our day.
Whether in schools, or on the roadways, or in the
theatre, the killing of innocent persons by the
deranged is a serious problem of our day. How is
this problem to be solved or at least mitigated?
Some solutions proposed have political roots, some
have human sincerity, while some have some merit.

The news report is all too familiar. There has
been another school shooting. Innocent children
have been killed for no reason whatsoever. Maniacs
or terrorists are playing god with innocent lives.
Why? What was accomplished? Why take their rage
and madness out on our pure, vulnerable youth?
They must be stopped! But how?

How are we going to control or eliminate
these acts of anger, hatred, and pure evil? It is not a
matter of whether we should do something. But
how? This madness has gone on for too long. Too
many children have been butchered.

Some politicians immediately cried out for
gun control. But it is only part of the answer. A

criminal can always get a gun. There are criminals who have lots of guns who are quite willing to sell them to other criminals. We have to strengthen and enforce the gun laws currently on the books. We also have to stop making assault weapons so easy to acquire. So, let's do it! And do it now! It won't stop it completely; but it will make it harder, and that's a start.

As I write, we are in the midst of a national student walk-out to protest the tragic shootings in Parkland, Florida, where 16 innocent students and a football coach lost their lives. It would have been justified if the students themselves had initiated the protest, but it was organized and strongly influenced by Women's March Youth Empower — left-wing supporters of the Democratic party. How wrong! While it is perfectly proper for any political party to demonstrate and push their agenda and platform, it is wrong to use children as pawns for their own purposes. I believe it would have been better to have the children pray for the deceased, for the mentally ill who acquire lethal weapons and unleash their violence on innocent children, and that this madness will disappear from our way of life forever.

Adults must recognize that this is a trauma for all American school-age children. Can you imagine a ten-year-old wondering if some maniac will burst through the door and start shooting him and his schoolmates? This is not what parents want their elementary school-aged children thinking about, and it is a serious problem. Taking frightened, innocent children, especially grammar-school children, and using them as political pawns is no solution. If anything, it is counter-productive, although it would appear to be productive for the organizers.

So, how are we going to put an end to this senseless butchering of our children? In my opinion, we have to stop the evil deeds of these people by trying to instill in them a solid sense of morality and self-discipline.

In 1942, in the middle of World War II, I was growing up in Toronto and won a scholarship to a prep school. I was a member of the school's cadet corps. I was 12 years old, standing at attention, and I could not scratch my itchy nose. I had to control my itch, all bodily sensations, and concentrate on the fact that I had been commanded to stand at attention. That was self-discipline and it has served me with tremendous benefit ever since. I am grateful for having had to learn self-discipline at such an early age and for the ability to employ it throughout my life to overcome obstacles and temptations.

So, how do we instill self-discipline to overcome the anger that seems to control these human beings that insist on killing young children?

Let me make a suggestion. Perhaps it is time to reinstitute the draft — eighteen months to two years of mandatory military service. There would be tremendous benefits for both the country and for the individual. The draftees would be trained to handle weapons. Some might even become teachers. They would also be subject to psychological testing, and potential killers may be detected and monitored.

I don't know if this will work. But nothing else seems to work. It won't hurt. It might even improve the probability of stopping the innocent carnage. We can't have any more of these situations. It broke my heart when I saw the pictures in the news of the butchered children. I am sure it did the same to you. It must be stopped!

THE TYRANNY OF
ENVIRONMENTAL PROTECTION

"We won't have a society if we
destroy the environment."
— Margaret Mead

The environment must be preserved. There are certainly excesses that must be curbed. But some of these excesses come from the environmentalists. Common sense is what we need, not coercion or dictatorial control. The penalty for failure is too great. You are needed for this effort.

In the name of environmental protection, government agencies world-wide have instituted a tyranny of absurd regulations. For example, the coal industry of the United States has been all but decimated and coastal areas find it difficult or impossible to maintain proper sea lanes for shipping. The whole world is now captivated by the belief that global warming is due to carbon emissions. Perhaps it is true, or perhaps not. It is true that the planet is getting warmer. But global warming also occurred in the 9th and 10th centuries. At that time, it would have been hard to blame it on carbon emissions from automobiles and industrial pollution. There is also evidence that global warming is due to solar flares and disturbances on the sun, which cyclically generate significantly more radiation than is normally the case.

I was once a board member of The Vatican Observatory Foundation in Arizona. The Environmental Protection Agency (EPA) denied us a permit to build an observatory on Mount Graham in association with the University of Arizona because there were ten red squirrels on the peak of the mountain and we were told that building the observatory would disrupt the working habitat of the squirrels. It took ten years to overcome this objection. The observatory was built. The red squirrel population doubled.

I was also involved in the construction of a building along the Atlantic coast. The windows of this building were to face the ocean. The EPA denied the permit to build unless we changed the placement of the windows, so they would no longer face the ocean. We were told that unless we did so, the seagulls would see their reflections in the glass, think they were a part of a flock, would fly into the windows, and destroy themselves. Our laughter turned to tears when we found ourselves embroiled in a dispute that lasted several years to overcome this ridiculous ruling.

I have owned summer home on the Atlantic coast for 50 years. It's on a barrier island with access through a long causeway from the mainland. Only once in those fifty years was there a hurricane strong enough to cause the road to flood. Even though the flooding was not enough to close the road, it was decided to raise the road level by four feet, to the tune of millions. The work began two years ago, and completion has now been extended another two years.

The reason for the delay is that there are four osprey nests along a three-mile stretch of the road, and no work can be done from May through September to give the osprey eggs time to incubate and hatch. It was suggested that perhaps the osprey nests could be moved; but it is not known for certain whether the osprey egg production and hatching would be affected. When osprey nests are close to human industrial processes, however, the newly hatched ospreys will often fall out of their nests and be destroyed.

Osprey nests are also found on buoys located on waterways close to the ocean. It is against the law to interfere with these nests even if the nests interfere with water traffic lights and signals. One the other hand, baby ospreys nesting on the buoys often fall out of the nests and drown.

Those associated with marine traffic know that dredging is an important aspect of maintaining seaways, but dredging permits are incredibly difficult to obtain.

Do we need to protect the environment? Yes, we do. We are stewards of the planet and we need to take care of it. But, let's be reasonable. The human race also occupies this planet and we need to provide for our children, keep ourselves fed and warm; build homes and safe roads and waterways to enable travel and trade with our fellow humans throughout the world. We can find ways to build our infrastructure, burn fuels safely and cleanly, keep our waterways safe, and protect our wildlife without endless delays imposed by the EPA.

Do we need to protect the environment? Yes! But let's use some common sense. Let's work with the EPA and find a balance between human need and the needs of our fellow creatures. The tyranny environmental protection is definitely not needed. Environmental protection — yes! Tyranny — no!

THE LUDDITES ARE UPON US

"I am not a Luddite. I am suspicious of technology. I am perfectly aware of its benefits, but I also try to pay attention to some of the negative effects."
— Neil Postman

I hope you are not a luddite. Irreparable harm will come to our world if the luddites are victorious. It would be funny if it weren't so serious a threat.

This is a clarion call to arms for all the level-headed people of the world. The luddites, i.e., those opposed to technological innovation, are attacking! They wear various uniforms. One of the most vocal bands is masquerading as the savior of the world as the Environmental Protection Agency (EPA).

Their latest campaign is against nighttime lighting. They want this reduced. Their claim is that the animal population requires darkness at night and too much light interferes with their normal circadian rhythms. They not only want to curtail the amount of light, but also the kind of light that we use — especially light emitting diodes (LED). Even though the electricity required to generate light in this fashion is significantly lower than what is used for traditional tungsten bulbs, the EPA claims that they still emit too much light and their use must be curtailed.

The Luddite movement emerged during the harsh economic climate of the Napoleonic Wars in the 18th century, which saw a rise of difficult working conditions in the new textile factories. Luddites objected primarily to the rising popularity of automated textile equipment, threatening the jobs and livelihoods of skilled workers as this technology allowed them to be replaced by cheaper and less skilled workers. When Fulton was demonstrating his steam engine, the luddites were marching to have it banned as a threat to the tranquility of their horses.

The luddites are now at work against the smartphone. They claim its use leads to addiction among the young. If it exists, it is not the phone creating the addiction, but rather parents using it as a babysitting device in order to bypass the responsibilities of caring for their children. The luddites also ignore how the smartphone has provided complete peace of mind by enabling parents to communicate with their children, 24/7, no matter where they are.

The luddites are simply everywhere. Now they complain that the electric car, a boon to clean air, is a threat to the environment because the electricity required will be generated by dirty fuels.

It's a wonder the luddites haven't tried to eliminate jet propulsion engines from airplanes. If you look up into the sky during daylight hours, contrails from jets flown at high altitudes are visible to the naked eye, and they contain a significant amount of pollution. Modern jets are more efficient, but there are many old airplanes still flying.

With all its harmful radiation, it's a wonder the luddites aren't complaining about the sun. Soon they will claim that we must send missions to remove the sunspots. I wonder how they're going to do that?

CITIZENSHIP

"When you single out any particular group of
people for secondary citizenship status, that's
a violation of basic human rights."
— Jimmy Carter

Citizenship is a technical way of making us members of the family. In ancient times, when populations were small, a nation consisted of members of the same family. Hence as populations grew, the nation became a tribe, then several tribes, and on and on until we arrive at the nations of today, some with over a billion people. Yet these nations have many things in common, usually tied to the history of those people groups. Hence the nation, to a large extent, is a family. Citizenship, then, is a way of joining the family. It carries responsibilities as well as benefits. Family membership also implies responsibility.

What does it take to be a citizen in any country? The easiest way is to be born there. Failing that, every country has a set of rules, whereby you enter the country, stay there for a certain period, obey its laws, and are eventually permitted to become a citizen.

147

Becoming a citizen of any country should invoke a sense of love and gratitude to the nationals and government of that country for granting citizenship. Citizenship implies not only a sense of gratitude, but a sense of responsibility. Citizens of democracies are responsible for electing representatives to enact laws which then govern the behavior of all citizens in that country to protect the common good. Laws then, are based on the will of the people, and citizens are expected to keep them, not circumvent or break them.

Many people enter the United States illegally. They then have difficulty in finding employment since documentation of citizenship is required, and such documentation is easy for a legal immigrant or citizen, but difficult if not impossible for illegal immigrants. Hence, illegal immigrants can rapidly become victimized by unscrupulous employers that will hire them at salary levels that legal immigrants or citizens would scorn. Such employers likely support any movement that would increase the number of illegal immigrants. But illegal immigrants are no benefit to the citizens at large, because by lowering the hourly rate of employment, they are doing a disservice to their fellow citizens. Illegal immigrants, then, are not good for the country, even though they may be good for unscrupulous employers who are seeking cheap labor.

Immigration laws in the U.S. are currently under a great deal of scrutiny and often bitter debate. One extreme seeks to deport illegal immigrants; and the other, to allow for open immigration. In the latter case, it means that the rules for admission of immigrants would be relaxed significantly so that illegal immigration would be eliminated, since everyone would be declared legal.

The extreme positions should be examined. If there is open immigration, the floodgates would be released, and the number of immigrants would become almost uncontrollable. Hence, the concept of open immigration isn't very sound. There should be some set of rules that regulate who can enter the country. Certainly, proven criminals should not be treated the same as those with no criminal record or suspected criminal intent. The minute you accept this premise, then the idea of open immigration would obviously be rejected.

Before going any further, I should admit that I am an immigrant. I was born, raised, and educated in Canada. I married an American and moved to the United States for my residence. I carried a green card as a landed immigrant, and at the appropriate time, became a citizen of the United States. I have dual citizenship. Hence, I sympathize with the immigrant who enters the United States with a desire to earn a living, to raise a family, obey the law, and become a U.S. citizen. That I hope would be the aim to all of those who seek to enter the United States. That should be the aim of anyone who seeks citizenship in any country.

People desire to live in certain countries because its citizens, over time, have expended considerable effort to build the country, and have paid considerable amount in taxes to create the type of environment and living conditions agreeable to those who wishes to enter the country. As a result, it is reasonable to expect that those who seek citizenship will also strive to improve the circumstances, the standard of living, and the wealth of the nation. This is often forgotten during the immigration debates in the United States, as well as in Europe and Asia where waves of refugees flow from country to country seeking residence.

I don't have the answers, but my heart bleeds for those who suffer. When I see images of boatloads of refugees finally making land, I am elated as a human being that they have been rescued from the perils and dangers of the sea and of their former home. And yet, my sense of justice asks why they must be a burden to the citizens of their new home. As human beings, of course we take care of our brothers. But as citizens, we ask why they should not bear their fair share of the burden of living in their new land. I can only ask questions and hope that reasonable people come to reasonable solutions.

One final point concerning citizenship. At age 12, I was a boy soldier in the Canadian army because I went to a military school where its cadet corps was a part of the Irish Regiment of Canada. The faculty advisor was one of our teachers, and he was also a Major in the Canadian Army. I was proud to wear the uniform of that cadet corps. I was proud to be a member of the Irish Regiment of Canada. My cousins served during WWII as part of the Canadian armed forces. My brother was an officer of the Canadian Army Dental Corps. We did not quibble, and we appreciated being able to do our bit. Standing at attention without the ability to scratch my nose at 12 years old gave me a sense of self-discipline. That self-discipline has served me nobly throughout my life.

I find it tiresome when I see highly paid athletes, all making well over a million dollars a year, refusing to stand when the national anthem is played. Who do they think they are? Do they know they are insulting the symbol of the society which allowed them the freedom to express themselves with their bad manners and ignorance, and pursue their dreams and earn more money than most of their fellow citizens can imagine? By all means protest, but please show respect for the symbol of the freedom that allows you to protest. Respect for the law includes respect for the mores, practices, and traditions associated with citizenship in every country. Their behavior is deplorable.

I am a citizen of the United States of America, with a stress on "United." I am proud to be one. I am willing to do all that I can to defend my fellow citizens. I will defend, obey, and uphold the laws of our country. I do so willingly and with pride.

I believe that is the true meaning of being "politically correct."

BASEBALL

"Love is the most important thing in the world,
but baseball is pretty good, too."
— Yogi Berra

I never played baseball beyond High School. In college, I was always too busy in the Spring with exams; and the Fall was taken up with football.

I loved playing baseball. I played second base. The hot spot. I think I can still throw a perfect strike from second base to home. I did it one day about two years ago with one of my grandsons, Jack. He was totally surprised. So was I!

I played baseball in grade school and high school. Then I played again with my sons when I was their Little League Coach. It is the same kind of strategy that is needed to be successful in business. I strongly advise you to do the same. Success comes from doing such things as picking the players you think will get on base. It can be that simple. Of course, it goes on from there.

Baseball is a game of strategy. It is the same kind of strategy needed to be successful in any kind of endeavor. If the goal is to win according to some measure of performance, then baseball strategy will do the trick. Think for a moment. In baseball victory is established by the plurality of runs. But to get runs, you have to get runners on base, and you have to advance them around the bases to home. In addition, you have to keep the other team from doing that same thing. The strategy comes with the way you manage your players while defeating the opposition.

For those spectators who don't know what is going on, it may even appear to be boring. I have played baseball myself and managed baseball in the Little League circuit. There is always a lot of excitement in both. Let me tell you why.

I started playing baseball as a squirt in grade school. Because of my small stature, teammates and fans would shudder every time I came to bat. Occasionally, I would hit the ball just hard enough to outrun the ball to first base. I was fast, but the ball didn't get very far. That didn't happen too often; but at least I never struck out.

Retribution came during my freshman year of high school. The summer between eighth grade and high school, I grew four or five inches and gained more than twenty pounds. I had a batting average of .597 that year, and I was homerun king of our intramural league. I went back to my grade school one afternoon and was invited to come up to home plate and hit. I hit the ball over the school building which was at the back of the ball field. The coach said: "Why couldn't you hit the ball like that when you were here?" I laughed and said, "Because I was a little runt." So, strategy number one in baseball: Make sure you don't have any runts on your team! Remember, though, they do eventually grow up!

I remembered that lesson very well when I was coaching Little League. I had a strike out champion on the team, a kid called Charlie. I never lost faith in Charlie. He had the right stance and the right swing but somehow, he never connected with the ball. I didn't pull Charlie. I let him go for his regular at bat, even though I knew it would cost the team an out. Then, one day, Charlie connected. He hit a homer! From then on, Charlie hit often and long. My faith in him was justified. And I remembered myself as a little runt, rarely given the chance to see what I could do. So, rule number two: Give your players a chance!

I see Charlie occasionally. He has his own children now who are playing baseball in Little League. Whenever I see him, we reminisce and laugh. I was both fortunate and unfortunate to coach my own sons in Little League. It was a great joy but because I put my sons in positions where I thought they would be most effective, other parents criticized me, claiming that I was exercising nepotism. Nothing could have been further from the truth. My sons displayed their ability and stifled the criticism. Rules Number 3, 4, and 5 in baseball and in life: do your best, use your best judgement, and ignore the peanut gallery.

During the years that I coached Little League, girls were permitted to play. What a joy! The girls were usually bigger than the boys. They hit the ball harder and farther. That gave the boys the incentive to improve. It was a win-win situation.

It just so happened one year that my team won the championship and then played against the champions of another local league. We were called the Yankees and were members of the Wayne Little League. We went to the championship game — a one-game playoff for the regional championship against the neighboring baseball organization, the Radnor Little League. My son Paul was the leadoff hitter for our team. Lo and behold, the pitcher was Toby, Paul's best friend. Toby's yard backed up to ours and Toby spent as much time in our house as Paul spent in Toby's. The game began and there was Toby, pitching for the Radnor champs. The boys fell down laughing in disbelief.

Toby pitched to Paul but couldn't seem to hit the strike zone. Paul was walked on four pitches. We won that game. Afterwards, I asked Toby, "How come you couldn't throw a strike when Paul was at bat?" Toby laughed, "You try it!" He was referring to the fact that Paul was quite small at the time. Not anymore!

The idea is to win, of course. We did! But even when we lost the game, we always won. Playing baseball is a lot of fun and I believe Little League is one the best programs we have to offer our youth. It teaches boys and girls how to play the game, how to play as a team, and how to give everyone on the team a chance. Someday those little runts called boys will grow up. Who knows what they will become? But you can be sure of one thing — that as they grow bigger and stronger — they will hit the ball further and further!

GREAT CITIES

"A great city is that which has the
greatest men and women."
— Walt Whitman

Travel is broadening – in experience and often in the hips. I have been fortunate to travel extensively during my professional career and I believe there are some cities on the planet that can be considered outstanding places to live.

This is a short look at what good strategy can lead to. Travel is an integral part of most businesses today. For me, it was more than that. My clients were around the world. I often was on an airplane each day of the week. It gave me an opportunity to visit on more than one occasion the principal cities of the world. Here are some of my reflections on a few of them.

First, of course, there is my hometown of Toronto where I grew up in the 1930s. It was a small city then — at most, half a million people. But because of WWII, and the immigration flood that occurred afterward, Toronto became a cosmopolitan city. Canada in turn, went from a nation of 11 million people to one of 35 million today. Toronto and its environs — 12 suburbs — were united in

1949 into metropolitan Toronto by House Bill 80 of the Ontario Legislature. Metropolitan Toronto blossomed and exploded. Today, Toronto is a city of over 400 square miles and a population nudging up against that of Chicago — 4.5 to 5 million people. What makes Toronto unique is its modern buildings, its cleanliness, its safety, and the courtesy of its people, especially the police force. Today, you are perfectly safe to ride a subway in Toronto into the wee hours of the morning.

Then there's London. What can I say? It's historic, it's cosmopolitan. In many ways, it's the crossroads of the world, and I am quite fond of it. Although battered with bombs during the Second World War, today it is practically the commercial capital of the world. I often liked to walk and look out for the daily horse guard parades in St. James and Hyde Parks. Barbara and I had an apartment for some years in Knightsbridge, in the West End. We could walk to the Oratory, to Harrods, and to Royal Albert Hall to attend concerts and the opera; or we could take a twenty-minute cab ride to the theater district where we attended various plays and performances. Old Vic was a bit further on across the river where we attended productions of Shakespearean plays, or those by Christopher Marlowe. London offers so many kinds of attractions. The parliament buildings are quite special, soaked in history of so many eras. The Tower of London, of course, is replete with history. Such is London — history personified.

Rome is also one of my favorite cities. Who can describe Rome in words? Dante perhaps? But the history — you can walk along the street, see a public fountain, read the inscription, and discover it was created by Michelangelo! And then there's the food — I have never had a bad meal in Rome in all the years that I have traveled there. Everywhere there is grandeur, history, art, and the joy of the people. That's Rome!

Ah… Paris. Full of life, you almost feel as if music is playing as you walk the streets, and often, it is! Paris itself is full of history, but it is more the atmosphere and the joie de vivre of the people that permeates the streets. The people themselves are fun to watch in Paris — especially the women and the way they dress. Trés chic!

Montreal is what Paris must have been a couple of centuries ago, with a little bit of modern mixed in. It also has the snow in the winter, lots of it, and you can ski on Mont Royal right in the heart of the city. It is enchanting to dine on the top floor of *Place Ville Marie* and feel like you are smack dab in the middle of a blizzard. Yet you are warm, comfortable, and enjoying a four-star meal!

Vancouver sits in the foothills of the majestic Rocky Mountains and it is a cross between the orient and what was once the orderly nature of the British Empire. It lies across the bay from Victoria which must have been London in the 19th century. Both are beautiful gems on the Pacific coast of Canada.

Los Angeles exploded and has sprawled all over hundreds and hundreds of square miles. The first time I arrived in Los Angeles I asked for a map of the city and was handed a book. Each page was a different section of the city. It certainly is an exciting place to visit.

Then there is San Francisco — one of my favorites of anywhere in the world. San Francisco is a world unto itself. The ambiance is varied, the restaurants are unbelievably good, and the people would march anywhere to fight for the rights of cats. San Francisco can only be described as exciting and a great place to visit.

I'll end my list of great cities with New York. I lived in New York for about three years and worked in and around New York for another ten or fifteen. There is no parallel anywhere for the stateliness, the grandeur, or the excitement of New York. The song "New York, New York" says it all.

I was one of those strange people that enjoyed living in New York. I miss it. I miss many of these cities as I now live in suburban Philadelphia.

And what about my current hometown of Philadelphia? At this stage in my life, I wouldn't live anywhere else.

THE OVAL OFFICE

"I've worked for four presidents and watched two
others up close, and I know that there's no such
thing as a routine day in the Oval Office."
— Dick Cheney

The first time I saw the Oval Office I was
surprised at how small it was. In fact, it is somewhat
cluttered. The President's desk is in front of the oval
windows. The actual desk and the size of the desk
depends upon the President in power at the time.

My first visit to the Oval Office was when
George H.W. Bush, or Bush 41, was President. I
think it must have been 1990. I was part of a group
of board members of the National Italian American
Foundation that was being briefed by President Bush
that day in the Roosevelt Room. President Bush's
briefing ranged throughout the entire world,
highlighting our national interests and involvement.
He was superb. He then invited each of us
individually for a photo opportunity in front of the
fireplace in the Oval Office. He was most gracious
in his comments and in welcoming us.

Later that day we had lunch in the
congressional lunch room and I was further

privileged to sit beside the speaker of the house at the time, Tom Foley from Washington.

I have been in the Oval Office on other occasions and my first impression has not been changed. It is remarkably small for the office of the most powerful man in the world. And yet the size is immaterial. There is an essence to the oval office that transcends anything other than the fact of simple words "the Oval Office".

Equally impressive and awe-inspiring are the words Sala Clementina. This is the conference room where the pope conducts most of his private audiences. I've been in that room scores of times. I've met with three of the popes repeatedly. These were St. John Paul II, Benedict XVI, and Francis. I have also met with them in the Paul VI auditorium. Far more impressive I have met with St. John Paul II in his private apartment. Barbara and I were blessed beyond belief to have attended mass in the private chapel of St. John Paull II four times. On one of those occasions Barbara was one of the readers.

What's it like to talk on a one-to-one basis with the Pope or the President? It's exhilarating in one sense, but it leads to an understanding that we are talking to a man. He has the same problems that we have but on a different scale or magnitude. The one feature that stands out in my mind in all of these encounters is the graciousness of these individuals. With President Bush he happened to notice the tie I was wearing that contained the emblem of the Order of the Holy Sepulchre and we engaged in conversation as he probed deeper and deeper in to what the Order was and what it stood for and what it did. He exhibited a profound depth of interest and as we proceeded in our discussion he was relating what I told him about the Order to his knowledge as to what was going on in the world at the time. The conversation was spirited.

Our conversations with the Popes were equally spirited. St. John Paul II had the habit of taking one hand from each of us and creating a circuit of the three of us as one. He always asked about our children. He was always extremely enthusiastic about our cardinal in Philadelphia, his great friend Cardinal John Krol. As he came to knows us he would automatically talk about Cardinal Krol or Philadelphia or something unique that showed that he was well aware of what was going on in different parts of the world.

With Benedict his love came through. He is a kind and loving man.

Pope Francis too is a man full of love which he exudes as you talk to him. We were blessed to be the first group and private audience with him after his election in 2013. We were in the Sala Clementina and he came in through the front as is usually the case when the audience is in that chamber. We went up to him as a couple and had the chance to talk to him personally. He was most gracious. We spoke in Italian. Then when the audience was done and instead of exiting from the front of the room he walked directly to me, we talked a little and shook my hand then went out the back door of the room. That was Francis.

We were given a tour of the papal apartments by Cardinal Harvey, who for years managed the Papal Household. The apartments had been refurbished through a grant from the board members of the Papal Foundation.

I feel I was privileged to have such opportunities.

GOVERNANCE

"Sustainable development is the pathway to the
future we want for all. It offers a framework to
generate economic growth, achieve social
justice, exercise environmental stewardship
and strengthen governance."
— Ban Ki-moon

The world is changing in many ways. I think
it is mainly because of the instant communication
capability that we have. For those connected,
anything can be made known to anyone, anytime.
Soon, with the entire world connected, anyone in the
world can instantly be informed of anything. Think
for a moment what that means. Again – anyone,
anywhere, anytime, anything. What a power for
control. Fairly often, that information is wrong, fake,
or used as a means of formulating and controlling
public opinion.

Elsewhere in this book I comment on the use
of propaganda with lies to distort the truth and
control the reaction of the public. For now, let me
recall that the technique of the "big lie" was used for
evil purposes by the Nazis in Germany, and most
especially by their propaganda minister, Dr. Joseph
Goebbels.

On a more interesting side, I well remember saying those words to Pope St. John Paul II in 1991 or so in New York. We were at the Path to Peace office in New York where we had arranged for a demonstration of the rudimentary internet we had in those days. I can still visualize the twinkle in his eye as he smiled and asked "Anytime?". We answered "Yes." Then with a chuckle added to the twinkly, he added "Anyone?" After our repeated "Yes", he added a broad grin to the twinkle and chuckle, as he said "Good!"

I know he used the internet. I can just imagine the chuckle as he zinged some bishop or cardinal.

But humor aside, think carefully of the implications. What if some organization can influence the thinking of hundreds of millions, if not billions, of people? What if some organization could listen in to all your conversations, record every word you utter, and steer comments to enhance, manage or change your opinions on issues of interest to the organization's agenda? What if the organization is the government? What if that organization is a super corporation with vast powers and resources of finance and technology giving the directors of such corporations, immense power? What if that power could influence the laws under which you lived?

In the United States we have a written Constitution with a written Bill of Rights included. We have a system of government with a separation of powers which prevents a dictatorship taking power. Is that true today?

Consider the situation. Our Constitution separates the powers and processes of government into the legislative which makes the laws, the Executive which enforces the laws, and the Judicial which interprets the validity of the laws and their application of the rules and punishments of those who break the laws that are deemed constitutional.

In our recent history, the actions of the Executive branch of government have gone far beyond what the framers of the Constitution foresaw. Over the past hundred years, the Executive branch of government expanded almost exponentially, and the Presidents began issuing rulings that became a vehicle for making law. The Judicial in turn in its rulings soon assumed the role of creating law. The result is the current situation where the Judicial branch of government has almost usurped the role of the legislative branch of government.

Under attack are the basic freedoms of the Bill of Rights. Secularism promulgated by Court Rulings is rapidly reducing the impact of the Bill of

Rights in our daily lives. This is true in Europe even more so that in the United States. The Court rulings now define marriage, sex, freedom of speech, freedom of religious observance, and the right to life. For example, while freedom of worship is promulgated, the actual practice and display of that practice is often smothered. Religious symbols are prohibited if they offend. Public prayer is prohibited in public places. There is great danger that the Bill of Rights will soon become whatever the Courts decide. It seems ironic that the Courts that place so much emphasis on precedent totally ignore history and the tradition of religious freedom that was the cornerstone of the flight of the immigrants to these shores to become the United States of America.

Marshall McLuhan predicted the rise of the Global Village. What he didn't predict was the tyranny of the those suppressing any opinions or actions contrary to their efforts for control. Control of the internet and modern means of communication may very well become the battle ground of the future.

LIFE, LOVE, AND MARRIAGE

"In my long life I have found peace, joy, and happiness beyond my fondest hopes and dreams. One of the supreme benedictions of my life has been my marriage to an elect daughter of God. I love her with all my heart and soul."
— James E. Faust

I could not have said it better. But let me add a little item of importance. Love includes bringing to the table, so to speak, your contribution to the marriage. In my case, it is 57 years of partnership. We also faced some tough situations. They involved life and death. I am sure you too will face, and probably have faced, similar situations. These guidelines of what we did hopefully will be of help to you.

Love is the lubricant that makes the bumps throughout a marriage glide by. Love is the yearning to be with the person you love, to be in union — to be one. I love Barbara, my children, my grandchildren, my great-grandchild, and my many friends. I hate to be separated from them. But my career involved a lot of travel to cities all over the world; and I had no choice.

Barbara has put up with much during our marriage. We have been married 56 years, and during that time I'd been away thousands of nights. One year I calculated that I spent 100 nights out of town. There isn't a major city in the world that I haven't visited — some of them many times. I commuted to London like I was going downtown. I was in Rome so many times I considered buying a villa there. Paris was another frequent flier destination, not to mention Vienna, Munich, Moscow, Frankfort, Milan, and so on. In North America, I've been to most of the states and to all the provinces of Canada. I've been to Mexico, the West Indies, the Bahamas, Bermuda, and as for the islands, I've been to Hawaii, Majorca, Sicily, Rhodes, and Malta. Of course, one of the advantages of all this travel was the ability to take Barbara on some interesting trips and vacations. On our honeymoon, we took a transatlantic cruise, and then spent five more weeks in Europe before heading home.

But love and marriage are much more than traveling with your bride and I have many great memories of our lives together. I remember living in New York and coming home from work to our apartment on the 21st floor to find Barbara waiting at the door with Peter, our first of four sons. She had my arrival times down pretty well. Peter would be all excited to see daddy. He would show off by crawling along the hallway and I would laugh my head off when he would crawl out of his diaper. Peter was always energetic as a baby and to this day, he has a lot of energy.

I think elsewhere I wrote about the joy of rocking the babies to sleep. Holding a baby is an inexplicable joy and happiness. I had the privilege of holding each of my children and grandchildren shortly after they were born. Looking into the eyes of a new baby is an unbelievable experience of sheer gratitude and joy. Isn't that what love is all about? Life is an exercise of love. Without love, how can there be life? Or rather, how can there be a life that is full? Certainly, there can be life without love, but I don't understand how.

Life is an adventure. Just living and loving, sharing, being grateful, sensing the love of family and relatives and the comradery of friends is indescribable. So, I can't understand anyone who would condone or have an abortion. How can a living person destroy another living person and deny them the opportunities that they themselves enjoy — with no remorse or understanding that the destruction of human life is the greatest of sins? There can be no satisfaction in taking an innocent human life. I shudder when I contemplate the late-term abortions where the abortionist kills the child after it is born.

Lest you think I never faced such a decision, let me tell you about the birth of our son Peter. In 1963, Barbara was diagnosed with German measles in the sixth week of her pregnancy. Abortion had not been legalized, but there were many abortion mills functioning even at that time. Our doctor recommended an immediate therapeutic abortion, stressing the fact that the baby would be born deficient in many ways. We decided to change doctors. At the time, I was the Chief Information Officer of Olin Mathieson, a conglomerate that owned Squibb among other companies. I went to the medical director and she directed me to Dr. Robert Cushing, an eminent gynecologist, and at that time, adviser to the Mayor of New York on such issues. He agreed with our decision against an abortion and delivered Peter without incident. Throughout his schooling, Peter had a greater than 4.0 average, attended the U.S. Naval Academy and served in the Submarine Service. There is nothing abnormal about Peter except perhaps for his energy and aptitude. How many geniuses are robbed from their service to humanity by decisions for an abortion. How many Einsteins, Mozarts, Jobses, or Gateses have we lost?

The threat to life extends to the aged, helpless, and infirm. Instead of honoring our most vulnerable citizens, efforts are being waged to deny them life. Whether to balance the healthcare budget, or out of a misguided belief that they would be spared pain, legislation will be sought first for assisted suicide, and soon after, for euthanasia. Wherever such practices have become common, as in Holland and Belgium, abuses have set in and quite often patients are euthanized without their consent. In Holland, some 5,000 or more people each year have been terminated without their permission. In the United States, Oregon has passed such legislation. Other states are not far behind.

In Europe, 14-year-old boys have been known to make such decisions and in Belgium, there is no age limit for those seeking assisted suicide. There are many naïve and well-intentioned people who are fooled and push for such legislation. Beware! They may have their eyes on you.

"Life is Worth Living," was an inspirational American television series which ran in the 1950s, featuring the Venerable Archbishop Fulton J. Sheen. Life is not only worth living, it should be guaranteed and protected. We have a responsibility to protect those that are given to our charge. A doctor has a responsibility to do everything possible to prolong the life of his patients, in a way that is free of pain and difficulty. Quite often that is impossible. I have been in severe pain after major surgeries. I have been on the verge of death at least five times. I have been anointed 13 times with the Sacrament of the Sick by a priest of the Roman Catholic Church. I have suffered through a heart attack, major surgeries, lethal cancer, and I have survived them all. I was told regarding my cancer to get my affairs in order because I had very little time left. I was told I had anywhere from months to two years left. I made a pilgrimage to the shrine at Lourdes, France as a *malade* (a sick person) with a doctor's judgement that it was my last hope since my cancer would kill me shortly. Yet I returned from Lourdes and a year later was cancer free. The doctors called it a miracle. I called it the power of prayer. Thanks Mom!

I believe that I have had a blessed life. I have been surrounded by an envelope of love which protected me through many perils. I have been struck by lightning in an airplane. I have been aboard airliners that had to abort take-offs and landings — once landing in a cornfield. I have been catapulted off a Navy aircraft carrier.

I have been blessed with a tremendous marriage. My wife Barbara is a saint in many ways. I kid her that she will be canonized because she has put up with me, but I think she will be canonized because she truly is a saint. I am grateful for Barbara, for her parents who raised such a wonderful girl, for my parents, for all our children, family, friends, and most especially for my mother, whom I think is still looking after her little boy.

I am grateful every day for the many gifts given to me and for the goodness, love, and care that has surrounded me all my life. Yes. I can say that I have lived a blessed life.

SUNSETS

"I don't know what you could say about a day in which you have seen four beautiful sunsets."
— John Glenn

The sunset is the end of the day. If you are orbiting the earth, it measures another cycle. That becomes an important point. Is the sunset the end of the day, or just one of many circuits of the Earth. This is just another way of looking at the sunset. It is a way-point for your success or failure in some endeavor. If a success, accept it and move on. If a failure, consider it a way-point, and push to convert it to success. As Yogi Berra was wont to say, "The game isn't over until the fat lady sings."

Sunsets can be glorious and can be seen from many vantage points. One of my favorites is from the flight deck of an airliner flying west over the ocean. Watching the sun set from the deck of a sailing ship is equally breathtaking. Their impact is enhanced by the motion of the boat and the sound of the waves slipping past the hull. A full sense of utter peace and contentment fills the heart and soul.

I have seen sunsets over the Atlantic Ocean, the Chesapeake Bay, Lake Ontario, and most startling of all, the Arctic Ocean. Quite often, just as the sun has set, the Aurora Borealis, or Northern Lights, illuminates the sky. Subdued slivers of green light streak the heavens. In the winter months, the Northern Lights often striate the endless darkness. The Northern Lights is a form of radiation as opposed to the spectral dispersion of light of a typical sunset. But no matter the science behind them, they promise the sun will rise the next day, despite the length of the night.

I have also seen sunsets from various cities around the world. In the early years of our marriage, Barbara and I lived in Forest Hills, New York, on the 21st floor of a building with a terrace overlooking New York City. Sunsets in New York are especially brilliant because of all the dust particles in the air. Night after night we would sit on our terrace, intoxicated with the dazzling array of color that backdropped the Empire State Building.

But of all the sunsets I have ever seen, I was able to photograph my favorite from the Yacht Club of Sea Isle City, New Jersey. The sun descended over the intercoastal waterway, across the wetlands and into a magnificent display of color through the atmosphere. I framed the print and called it "By Rocky and by God."

I believe sunsets are the promise of tomorrow. When granted a glimpse of a magnificent one, I am often inspired to let go of all the bad things that may have happened that day, or to at least ignore them. They inspire me to reflect upon my life, and upon the things I have done for others. The financial reward that we achieve in life is nothing compared to the gracious smile of an older person whom you have helped or consoled, or the smile on the face of a child whom you love. Just as it promises the sun will rise the next day, a setting sun is a metaphor for the promise of something eternal. There is an ethereal beauty and dignity intrinsic to a sunset, just as the sunset years of one's life are often the most beautiful. The work day is over. Enjoy your sunset.

DEATH

"While I thought that I was learning how to live,
I have been learning how to die."
— Leonardo da Vinci

The common end for all of us is death. But death is not necessarily the end. It's all in the manner that we consider it. Death can be a terminal point – the junction of the next start, or truly the final stop. The definition depends on what motivates you before the final curtain. Do you take bows afterwards, or just leave the curtain closed? The best approach is to never lose hope that this is not the final curtain at all.

It is difficult to picture one's own mortality, but I have faced death many times in my 89 years — twice before the age of four. I have been anointed thirteen times, four of them when death seemed imminent. On one occasion, I believed I was dead, but I wasn't. So, let me begin with that story.

In September of 2016, I was operated on for bladder cancer at the University of Pennsylvania. This was my thirteenth surgery in six years and this time, the surgeon, Dr. Bruce Malkowicz, prepared me for not surviving the operation. After all the surgeries, he had become quite a friend. He explained that he might have to remove my bladder and that it might kill me. He was less than sanguine about my chances. I had been bleeding for six weeks and nothing succeeded in stopping it. I received four blood transfusions during that time. There was some hope, however. A new treatment for bladder cancer was available that boosted the body's immune system to kill the cancer. I was a candidate for this immunotherapy so long as the bleeding could be stopped. Hence, the surgery had two objectives: stop the bleeding and locate the tumor.

As I was wheeled into the operating room, I wondered if I would come out of the surgery alive.

When I awoke, I was alone in a 40x40 room. I had no catheter in me. This was totally unlike other surgeries when I was surrounded by people and family members. I thought I was dead. I remember thinking, "Is this what being dead is like?" I also assumed that my body had been put in this room prior to going down to the morgue. Then I spotted someone walking in the distance. I shouted, and a nurse came over. I said, "Where is everybody?" She answered, "They went to lunch." I said, "What!" Seeing my dissatisfaction with her answer, she continued, "We are waiting for transport. When it gets here, you are going to your room where your wife is waiting for you. Then you can get dressed and go home."

So, finally I was certain I was still alive. When I got to my room, my wife Barbara explained that the surgeon could not find the tumor. It was gone. I was free of cancer. My bleeding had been caused by my bladder separating from its lining, which was now floating inside my bladder. My bladder, in turn, had grown a new lining. My prayers and those of untold scores of friends who prayed for my recovery had been answered.

That was certainly a wonderful day for me.

There were days in the previous six years, however, that were less than stellar. The outcome was the same, in a sense, I remained alive, and for that, I am grateful. But believe me, there were tough days.

In the spring of 2011, I was surprised one day to see blood in my urine. I went immediately to a local urologist who examined me, found a tumor, and informed me that I required immediate surgery. I went home and researched the best surgeons for this procedure in the country. I made an appointment with one at Johns Hopkins in Baltimore. A week later, he removed the tumor and I went home the next day. A few days later, I received a copy of the biopsy report which stated I had high-grade invasive bladder cancer and that there were pieces of the tumor still there. I went back to the surgeon and he explained that the cancer would penetrate the muscle and lining of the bladder, escape into my body, and lead to extensive metastases of the cancer into different parts of my body. I asked him how long I had left, and he said two years or less. Then he refused to go in and remove the remaining tags of the tumor.

I then went to Sloan Kettering in New York to Dr. Guido Dalbagni who operated and removed the tags. But of course, the diagnosis was the same. He put me on a chemo treatment called BCG which was a TB vaccination. Two cycles of this had no effect. Then he put me on another chemotherapy, gemcitabine, which nearly killed me. Then he examined me and found I had two more tumors. He went in and removed them. Then the bleeding began, and I ended up in one emergency room after another. I was in and out of New York and Sloan with surgeries, bleeding, and cauterizations. Finally, he said he could do no more for me, except to remove my bladder. I went back to Hopkins, but now to a good friend, Dr. Jacek Mostwin. Jacek operated several times more while the bleeding cycle continued until he too, said he could do no more for me. We studied the scans together for hours, but Jacek explained the only possible solution was to remove my bladder, and that I would probably not survive the surgery.

He suggested I make a pilgrimage to Lourdes. He and I had been to Lourdes numerous times. We are both members of the Knights of Malta, a lay religious order. In fact, he is part of the medical commission, chairman at one time, that investigates the authenticity of miracles. I agreed and went in the spring of 2015, I went to Lourdes.

I then went back to Penn and to my dear friend and superb surgeon, Bruce Malkowicz. In September of 2016, during my thirteenth operation for bladder cancer, Bruce cut into my abdomen but could find no tumor. The trip to Lourdes, or prayer, or my body's immune system killed the cancer. The most rational explanation was that something triggered my immune system. I believe it was Lourdes and the power of prayer. Bruce thinks it was a miracle.

So, I am alive. But. I was face to face with mortality many times during those six years. It was disheartening, to say the least. I did not want to leave my family, especially my grandchildren. I wanted to watch them grow into adulthood. I also regretted work unfinished and books unwritten. Death was suddenly so real. I began thinking deeply about life and the hereafter and I wrote about it. But suddenly my spirits lifted, and I pushed on, ignoring the idea of dying. If I was going to die, there was nothing I could do about it except to continue to hope and fight. I did that. I hoped, I prayed, and I fought. I have never lost hope. I have always believed I would somehow pull through.

So, death – you are inevitable, but so be it. Until that day, I will live and never lose hope and confidence in a God that loves me. I also think my parents are still looking after their little boy. And of course, Barbara is a tower of strength, hope, and love. I have been blessed beyond all measure with the gifts given to me, especially my wife Barbara, of 57 years, and the gift of continued life.

Death is inevitable. I used to think sudden death was tragic. Not anymore. Now I think it is a blessing.

AFTERLIFE

"Do for this life as if you live forever, do for
the afterlife as if you die tomorrow."
— Ali ibn Abi Talib

The race isn't necessarily over if there is an afterlife. Bet on it. You have nothing to lose if you are wrong. But you may be right. The odds favor it.

The question of an afterlife has been debated throughout history. The Vikings called their version "Valhalla," or "hall of the slain," where they would prepare to one day continue their conquests alongside their god, Odin.

There were two basic thoughts on the afterlife described in the Bible during the time of Jesus. The Sadducees, or the Jewish aristocrats, did not believe in the afterlife, whereas the Pharisees, or the Jewish middle class, did believe.

The afterlife is a fundamental Christian belief, cemented by the death and resurrection of Jesus Christ.

What is the concept of an afterlife? Where does it come from? And how might it be perceived? In the 17th century, the scientist Blaise Pascal posed what he called the basic dilemma. Was there an afterlife or not? He suggested that you assumed that there was. If there was, then you win. And if there wasn't, then you lose nothing. This came to be known as Pascal's Wager.

Let's consider each one of us. We each have a body and a mind. But they do not distinguish us as persons. There is something more which leads us to do things in a specific way. For example, identical twins would not necessarily do the exact same thing the exact same way at all times. So, what distinguishes them? It is what we might loosely call personhood. For each of us, there is a driving force that leads us to excel and to make the decisions that we do. One aspect of this is our conscience which provides guidelines for choosing between right and wrong. But personhood is also that which makes us unique — in terms of what we like and don't like, what we say and don't say, what we do or don't do, and the impression that we make upon others. This "memory" remains alive even though our bodies and minds may have left the Earth.

For the Christian, personhood is wrapped up in the concept of the human soul. The soul is the essence of the person and includes the conscience. There doesn't seem to be much difference between personhood and soul, according to Christianity. The soul is spiritual, not corporeal, and it is Christian belief that the soul continues beyond the death of the body into the afterlife, until the end of the world.

How can we be sure that every person possesses a soul?

There have been apparitions throughout history of the Virgin Mary to certain chosen believers.

The most famous of these appearances occurred in Fatima in 1917 when 70,000 people saw the sun spin in the sky, then hurtle toward the earth before stopping. This miracle was foretold by the Virgin Mary to three peasant children who were privileged to see a vision of her on a number of occasions.

For me, the most touching of these apparitions occurred in 1531 when the Virgin Mary appeared to a native Mexican peasant named Juan Diego in what is now part of Mexico City. In a series of apparitions, she gave him messages to carry to his bishop. But the bishop did not believe Juan Diego and told him to ask the Lady for a sign to prove the apparitions were true. The Virgin told Juan Diego where he would find some roses blooming, even though it was the dead of winter. Juan Diego obeyed, found the roses, tucked them inside his cloak, and went on to see the bishop. When he opened his cloak to show the roses to the bishop, there was an image of the Virgin emblazoned on the cloak's lining. The bishop finally believed the messages from the holy Virgin. The cloak, with the Virgin's image, is now enshrined in the Basilica of Our Lady of Guadalupe in Mexico City. A close examination of the image shows Juan Diego's reflection in the irises of the Virgin's eyes, upside down, as it must be according to the laws of physics.

Another famous apparition of the Virgin Mary occurred in Lourdes, France, in 1858. Here the visionary was a young illiterate peasant girl named Bernadette Soubirous. She was commanded by the Virgin to dig in the earth near a garbage dump until she found a spring, then to wash her face in the scant muddy water. Each year, four to six million pilgrims visit the spring at Lourdes which has led to authentic miraculous cures on at least 66 occasions since 1858. These miraculous cures have been verified by a panel of medical doctors composed of Catholics, Protestants, and Jews. I can add one more to this total. I was suffering from a fatal cancer which was close to claiming my life when I went to Lourdes. I had been there many times before as a Knight of Malta, helping the sick who were praying for miraculous healing. Now I was one of the sick people praying for a cure for my own cancer. Within a short period of time after returning to the States, I was declared cured. The same surgeon who had previously performed numerous procedures on my bladder, opened me up and could find no tumor.

Was is a miracle? It certainly wasn't a medical cure. This was confirmed by some very famous and pre-eminent physicians.

So, we do have situations where those that have gone before us appear to certain chosen believers to help us on our way or to intercede for us in our daily struggles, or even cause miracles for tens of thousands to see.

Do you believe?

Is there an afterlife?

You decide.

EPILOGUE: MEMORIES

Come join my memories and add your own. I was motivated to keep plugging along. I never gave up on anything. That is the joy of these memories. I won! I am still here. I am on the right side of the grass. Come join me!

I have many memories. They date back to my time in the hospital when I was two years old. I didn't understand the doctors' words then, but I still remember them. They were discussing amputating my right leg. Apparently, I had a severe infection. In 1931, there wasn't much they could do with osteomyelitis. But I was lucky in my father. He insisted there had to be something that could be done other than amputation. Apparently, the doctor agreed and decided to try to scrape the infection off the bone. It worked. Thank God!

At the time, we lived in Hamilton, 40 miles southeast of Toronto, so I was taken to my Aunt Lena's house, which was closer to the hospital, to recuperate after being released. I remember I wanted my red firetruck. So, I will never forget the extreme joy when my uncle Donald walked into my aunt's house with my firetruck in his arms. He was my mother's oldest brother. Apparently, he made the 80-mile round trip to Hamilton, picked up the

197

beloved truck and drove it back to me. That is love, and it was reciprocated.

I also remember when I was four, and my father and a strange man that he called doctor were leaning over me. The doctor told my father that I would be dead the next day. Apparently, I had a fever of 107°F. Once again, my stubborn father refused to accept such desperate news. He contracted an ambulance and my mother and I were driven to a doctor that my father knew in Toronto, a Dr. Glionna. My father said he put a spray in my nose which must have been an early form of a sulpha drug. My fever broke, and I survived. Once again, thank God for my parents.

I also remember being happy sitting in our kitchen in Hamilton and all four of us throwing a ball around. I had an older brother, Jack, three years older than myself. We were real buddies.

We moved to Toronto when I was five. There are many memories associated with my brother. Walking to and from school each day, home for lunch and sitting with my mother and brother, talking about the things that happened at school. I especially remember the musicals in which the whole school participated. I remember vividly when I was in grade five or six, I was in a classical Negro musical. These were very popular in the 30's in Canada.

One of my most humorous childhood memories, although I wasn't laughing then, was my first effort at playing goal in hockey for the junior school team. I was about six or seven and the junior team did not have a goalie. I had often played goal with my brother's friends although I was a runt, three years younger, and they didn't know where to put me. So, they put me in goal. That day, when the junior team wanted me to play, I didn't have my skates, but agreed to play even without them. Wow! I couldn't move fast enough to stop the puck. I was scored on seven times. Every time I tried to move over to deflect the puck, I was hindered by my rubber boots. I should have thought to take them off and play in my socks. But that would have been strange and probably not allowed by the coach. Anyway, I made a comeback the next game, with skates, and I allowed no goals — a shutout! I could play goal pretty well since I had a lot of experience for my age, as long as I was wearing skates, that is. I had been playing goal since I was three or four years old. In Canada, we all turned our backyards into skating rinks and played hockey all throughout the neighborhood, as long as there was ice. My brother was also quite good, but he was essentially a defenseman. Our version of hockey consisted of one goalie — me — and everyone tried to score on me. That was good experience for the school games when I had some real defensemen.

I played goal throughout my school years. Every once in a while, I got fed up and played defense or left wing. I did rather well there but was most comfortable in goal. One time in high school, I got angry at the other team for scoring on me, grabbed the puck, skated up the ice and scored. The goal was disallowed because of some rule that said the goalie couldn't proceed beyond the blue line of the opposing team. I just laughed. To this day, I think it's one of the more humorous incidents of my sports career.

Those are the good memories. I also have some sad memories. The most traumatic is from walking up the stairs to bed one night when I was eight years old and found my mother lying on my parents' bedroom floor. It still brings tears to my eyes as I remember that scene. She had suffered a terrible miscarriage, two years before. They patched her together as best they could in 1936; but the doctors told my father she was extremely fragile, and she would not survive beyond two to three years. This was Tuesday, January 25th, 1938. She was 37. My mother was a kind lady. She was devastatingly pretty, with red hair and sparkling green eyes.

In those days, funerals were usually held at home. My mother lay in repose in our living room on Wednesday and Thursday and the funeral was Friday. I will never forget. I still today cannot imagine how hard it was on my 11-year old brother, and my father — a widower at 38. I clearly remember how he hugged us when we came home after the funeral. I never cried through that whole period. But three weeks later, I came home after school to any empty house and began to cry. It must have gone on for at least a half an hour.

It's tragic for a young boy to lose a parent, but somehow, it helped me when I became a parent. I have some wonderful family memories of holding each of our four boys in my arms and rocking them to sleep. There is a joy to holding a baby in your arms, especially when you know you had a role in his creation. It's an unbelievable moment to look down and see love reflected in the eyes of your child.

Feeding them was always an adventure. Sometimes it turned into hilarity, while I aimed the spoon for their mouths before it either dropped onto the floor or ended up in one of their ears. As I write this, I still remember and laugh. We always made sure there was always more food than we knew they would eat, because any one of the four would spill about as much as they ate during their early years.

I remember their accomplishments and victories — in the classroom, in the band, at the piano, or on the ocean — and then suddenly, or so it seemed, they graduated. All too soon, they left home and moved on with their own lives, careers, and families. I am a grandfather and great-grandfather now, but it's been a while, and it sure would be great to hold a baby in my arms again!

A couple of years ago, I wrote more fully of my Memories in a three-volume autobiography. The first volume is called, "Stories for My Grandchildren" and it spans the years from birth to my college days at the University of Toronto. The second volume is entitled "Scientist and Writer" and covers my careers in both those fields. The third volume is entitled "How I Changed the World," and recounts what led up to the invention of the smartphone, the invention itself, and the trials and tribulations which followed that changed the world but left me almost penniless. All three volumes are available through BlueNose Press on their website.

And now, saving the best for last, a few words about the love and center of my life – my wife Barbara. I remember the first time I saw her. I met her at a dinner party at the home of my business partner, John Mauchly. There was a knock at the door. I answered, and there she was. She was gorgeous. She was alive. She had a smile about her and a certain way of shaking her head that just endeared her to me. I remember the first time my father met her, he pulled me aside and said quietly "Grab her. She's gold!" And she is. I fell in love with Barbara at the Mauchly's front door, but I couldn't ask her out for some time because I traveled so much. Finally, we had our first date. We were married within six months.

We have been married fifty-seven years. We have four sons, aged 54 to 44, thirteen grandchildren, and one great grandchild. A marriage "blessed in heaven" as her mother used to say. It was indeed blessed in heaven and cemented in love.

I have always loved her. I always will.

ABOUT THE AUTHOR

ROCCO LEONARD MARTINO
BSc Mathematics & Finance '51
MASc Physics '52
UTIAS PhD Aerospace Engineering '56

Dr. Rocco L. Martino is the inventor of the CyberFone – the world's first smart phone – and the driving force behind the software systems permitting secure real-time video, voice and data linkages. Martino graduated Summa Cum Laude in Honors Mathematics and Finance from University College at the University of Toronto, and went on to earn a Master's degree in Physics and a Doctorate in Aerospace Engineering from the Institute of Aerospace Studies. His discovery of the heating factors during the re-entry of space vehicles led to the development of heat shields that made space travel possible today. He is the Founder and Chairman of the Board of Martino Systems, Inc. and U.S. Robots, Inc., and was the Founder, Chairman and CEO of XRT, Inc., a global leader in providing complete treasury, cash and banking relationship management solutions for many of the world's largest corporations and government entities.

Prior to founding XRT, Inc., Dr. Martino directed the Aerospace Division of Adalia, Ltd, a firm headed by Sir Robert Watson Watt, the inventor of Radar; directed all activities in Canada for UNIVAC, and worked with Admiral Grace Hopper on automatic programming systems; formed a partnership to create Mauchly Associates with Dr. John Mauchly, the co-inventor of computers, and spearheaded the Critical Path Method created by his company; served as the Chief Information Officer of the Olin Mathieson Corporation; and finally headed the Special Projects Group of Booz Allen and Hamilton.

Rocco Leonard Martino is also the author of five novels, twenty-six nonfiction books, as well as scores of papers and numerous corporate monographs on computers, communications, networks and planning.

He served as Professor of Engineering and Chair of the Systems Engineering Department of the University of Waterloo and as Professor of Mathematics at New York University.

Dr. Martino served on the boards of Saint Joseph's University in Philadelphia, the World Affairs Council, the Foreign Policy Research Institute (of which he is currently a Senior Fellow), the Gregorian University Foundation, the Vatican Observatory Foundation, the Order of Malta, and numerous other boards. He currently serves on the

Advisory Board of the University of Toronto's Institute of Aerospace Studies.

Dr. Martino has shared his good fortune with philanthropic works for handicapped children, merit scholarships at all levels in education, grants for cancer research, and building projects in higher education. An avid sailor, he captained his sloop "The Lady Barbara" in races in the mid-Atlantic. He served as Commodore and Board Chair of the Yacht Club of Sea Isle City, and Commodore and Secretary of the Mid-Atlantic Yacht Racing Association. He currently serves as President of the YCSIC Sailing Foundation. He is a member of the YCSIC, the Union league of Philadelphia, and the Overbrook Golf Club.

He has been honored by the Monte Jade Society, the National Italian American Foundation of Washington, and the CYO Hall of Fame in Philadelphia among others. He holds honorary doctorates from Gonzaga University (Spokane, WA), Neumann University (Aston, PA) and Chestnut Hill College (Philadelphia, PA), and was knighted by Pope St. John Paul II as a Knight of Saint Gregory. The Government of Canada granted him a personal Coat of Arms in 2003. In 2017 he was selected for enrolment in the Wall of Distinction of the Faculty of Engineering of the University of Toronto.

Dr. Martino's lifelong accomplishments have earned him a global reputation as a scientist, inventor, financial expert, technology guru, philanthropist and author.

www.ingramcontent.com/pod-product-compliance
Lightning Source LLC
Chambersburg PA
CBHW031250090426
42742CB00007B/389